Association Managers:

How To Avoid The Top 12 eLearning Mistakes That Sabotage Your Education Programs

Deborah C. Miller

MA, PMP, MOQ/OE

Association Managers:

How To Avoid The Top 12 eLearning Mistakes

That Sabotage Your Education Programs

Published by Miller Productivity.

Printed in the United States of America

ISBN: 978-1-939192-08-0

Limits of Liability / Disclaimer of Warranty

Additional Publications by Deborah C. Miller

Available from Amazon.com

Project Management: 7 Innovative Solutions
To Today's Project Challenges.

Simple Project Management Planning:
The Fundamentals For Project Success
Every Small Business Needs To Know (CD)

Business Continuity and Disaster Recovery:
Getting Ready Guide

Business Continuity and Disaster Recovery:
Getting Started Guide

Business Continuity and Disaster Recovery:
Putting It All Together

Lean Problem Solving: Cutting Through The Weeds To Increase Personal Productivity

Don't Get Left Behind:
A Personal Invitation from Deborah Miller

Because you bought my book I'd like to invite you to visit my blog and subscribe to receive updates so you can get the practical insights, tips and tools that I find valuable when providing eLearning services to my clients. I have also created a page on this website with all of the products and links I included in this book as an easy reference for you.

If you want to learn how to create eLearning courses that members love, explode your credibility with your members, and generate non-fee revenue, then here's what I'd like to invite you to do. Go ahead and log on to www.eLearningSecrets.com and sign up for a free account. It takes about 30 seconds and could very well revolutionize the results of your eLearning courses.

That means you'll be able to get all the latest developments in eLearning, as well as my latest tips, tricks and tools to leverage with your own eLearning courses (no matter what industry you are in). Again, signing up is easy and FREE. Point your web browser to www.eLearningSecrets.com and sign up for a free account (we promise never to spam or share your name with anyone).

So if you enjoyed this book and want to take your eLearning courses to the next level, head on over to www.eLearningSecrets.com right now and get onboard for free.

Table of Contents

Introduction

Welcome all Association Managers to "How To Avoid The Top 12 eLearning Mistakes That Sabotage Your Education Programs." I wrote this book based on my experience with managers and clients who make these same mistakes when developing eLearning programs for their organizations. I am often brought in to help fix the mistakes that were made because the Manager didn't understand the potential problems before they got started.

The mistakes here are actual problems based upon my own direct experience and the research I have conducted for my clients. These mistakes are real. If you are making even one of them, it can cost you and your Association a lot of money and wasted resources. Chances are you are making more than one of these. It's time to get a handle on these mistakes and fix them.

What We'll Cover

We are going to talk about the single biggest mistake people make with their eLearning programs. Why this is critical for your Association no matter what business you are in, and 12 specific mistakes people make and how to fix them.

Biggest Mistake

The single biggest mistake that I see Association Managers make is providing educational programs to their members that do not meet their needs. For many members, the most important reason to join an Association is the opportunity for personal and professional advancement through education. The education you create must provide value to your existing members. If done correctly your educational offerings can also be a compelling reason for new members to join.

Your goal as an Association Manager should be to identify the most valuable and relevant sources of content available and incorporate them to create your educational programs. Then you must deliver that content to your members using a variety of relevant delivery mechanisms.

To do this, you must understand the needs of your members and package your educational offerings in a way that is relevant, up-to-date, easy-to-access, and provides a reason for the members to consume the information. That means using the most up-to-date instructional design methods and technology.

It doesn't matter what industry you are in. These mistakes are being made in for-profit and non-profit organizations alike, manufacturing, health care, financial services and more. I have seen first-hand how poorly conceived and developed programs can hurt the organization's bottom line.

Why This Is Important

Training departments are rarely well funded and this mistake is more critical for a non-profit Association. The training is often viewed as an expense rather than an income-generating source of revenue for the organization. Yet, analysis shows that learning, (and eLearning in particular), can be one of the competitive advantages you can provide to your members.

In fact, the main growth area for eLearning is likely to be found in small companies and not-for-profit organizations. Typically, these organizations have a single person responsible for all eLearning activities. Because of this, the Association needs to be aware of the pitfalls they can face and the mistakes that are often made when implementing an eLearning program.

What This Means To You

It means that your members are relying upon your Association to provide them with the most relevant educational materials, packaged in a way that is easy to access and is going to help them achieve their goals. If your educational materials fall short of the mark, you will likely lose members and fail to attract new ones.

Penalties for Not Preventing or Fixing These Mistakes

The penalty for making these mistakes is that your organization is wasting precious resources. And I don't just mean time and money. The Association's reputation is at stake here, and if you are not seen as providing relevant and timely information that your members expect, your very existence could be in jeopardy.

I don't know of many Associations that have money to waste. In fact, most are looking for ways to enhance their non-fee revenue sources. Misusing and making these mistakes will negatively affect your bottom line.

How This Book is Different

The concept of eLearning is extremely simple: use a device capable of delivering online content/training to anyone, at any place, at any time. There are so many options it is difficult for people to evaluate the possibilities and to make a good decision for their organization.

What makes this book different from others you might have read is that I will give you my personal examples and the tools I use to get results. Some might say that talking about mistakes is being "negative." I disagree. When you know the pitfalls to avoid, and you can learn to recognize the traps ahead of time, you can save yourself a lot of time, frustration and money. Plus, we like to learn from examples. When we see examples of what not to do combined with solid advice on what to do instead, it creates a faster, more enduring learning experience. And when it comes to something as important as implementing eLearning in your Association, you can't afford to take one day longer than necessary to start getting results.

Let's stop wasting time and get right to the mistakes and how to avoid them.

Mistake #1: No Time To Strategize, I Need The Course Now!

What is the mistake?

A common mistake that Association Managers and others make is to jump into the eLearning course development without taking time to create a strategy and plan. If you don't take sufficient time upfront to strategize, you become committed to a process that will ultimately become your process for all subsequent course development activities. This may cause you to miss some critical steps or activities that ensure your course is a success.

Why it's a mistake

One of the advantages of planning is that you develop the big picture of where you want the eLearning program to go. For example, is this the first course in a series? If so, you will want to make sure you have a look and feel for the course that you are happy with and will want to use in the other courses as they are developed.

In addition, you will want to determine the best way to deliver the content so your members are getting the information they need in a logical manner. Haphazard course development often results in disjointed and confusing course offerings for members.

Another reason it's a mistake not to spend time in planning is that member needs are overlooked in the rush to get a course developed. If you are using course material from a subject matter expert, the original audience may be different from yours and the content may not fit the needs of your members.

It can also take a lot longer to develop a course if you have not completed some planning. Who will be responsible for the content? Who will approve the course? How will it be delivered? Will members pay to take the course? How will payment be handled?

If these questions are not answered upfront, delays can easily occur.

What are the consequences of making this mistake and how critical are they?

For smaller associations that are only going to provide a course or two, the consequences are less critical. However, if you are planning to offer a number of courses and have members pay for them, then the planning is crucial.

eLearning can be a big part of your member retention and acquisition strategies. If you develop courses that your members don't want to purchase or see as valuable, you are risking your membership development. The members might question your expertise in the industry. They may also question why they are paying to be a member if the quality of your courses are not up to their standards or expectations.

But more than that, you may be wasting time and resources in developing the courses that are taking the organization in the wrong direction—away from member expectations and needs.

Think about planning as a way to provide a roadmap for your eLearning trip. You want to know the destination and stops along the way before you begin packing. It's important to know who is going on the trip and what they need to have a great experience. Have they been there before? If so, what was their experience? Why are they going on the trip in the first place? Is it for pleasure or work? Understanding the reasons why they are on the trip and their expectations makes it a lot easier for you to provide them with the kind of experience they are looking for.

Why and when do people tend to make this mistake?

Not creating a strategy and plan is an easy mistake to make because most of us don't like to plan. We want to get it done and move on. Maybe in the past we have had a bad experience in planning where it took too long to get the plan done and then no one actually implemented the plan. I have seen organizations work for weeks to create a very detailed plan and then put it in a binder on the bookshelf and never look at it again.

Another common reason is that eLearning seems to be an easy concept and people don't realize that it is much different from creating traditional learning programs. It's really important to "begin as you plan to go" when planning your first course. Taking the time to know the difference between traditional learning and eLearning and what is required to implement a successful program is very important.

Occasionally, an association will have training staff who have created learning projects in the past. The assumption is that since they know about developing courses, they can naturally develop eLearning courses. There are some major things that make eLearning different enough that getting help from someone with eLearning experience is important.

And then there are the folks who have taken a couple of eLearning courses from another organization or university and think it looks easy so it shouldn't be very hard for them to implement in your organization.

Finally, people don't realize that help is available. Large and small consulting firms and individuals are available to help you to plan and develop your first course. Some are more expensive than others. A large consulting firm may not be appropriate for a small or medium sized association due to the cost. An independent consultant or small consulting firm may just be what you need. Nor should you feel obligated or restricted to use local resources. With the abundance of technology in today's world that allows workers to be remote, you can hire a great resource from almost anywhere.

Let me tell you a quick story to illustrate this point...

I've been guilty of this mistake myself. Let me tell you a quick story about my first experience developing a course without a plan. I was asked to develop an eLearning course for an organization. The course was currently being taught by a subject matter expert and he had a PowerPoint presentation that he used. He didn't have any notes, just the slides.

The project manager expected me to use exactly what was on the PowerPoint slides to create the storyboard and narration for the course. I sat through the physical training class to learn how the course was delivered. And then I went to work developing the eLearning course. First problem that I encountered was that the subject matter expert did not have examples that were relevant to the new audience. All of his examples were based on a different industry and were very specific to that audience. I didn't realize that until the project manager came back to me and wanted the course rewritten for his audience. Not planning was a huge time waste.

The second issue came when the project manager told me the course would not be presented as a PowerPoint show but they wanted it delivered as a screen-capture video. That required an additional rewrite as the medium being used was not compatible with the course design. Another big waste of time.

Had I had taken the time to ask questions and plan, the course would have been easier to develop and would have required fewer revisions and changes.

What should you do instead?

Always take the time to strategize, no matter how experienced you are with the organization or in developing eLearning programs. It's better to take a day or two to understand upfront what the requirements are than to have to spend time and resources to redo the work.

Understand the purpose for the courses you are developing. Why are you providing them to your members? What results do your members want as a result of taking your course? An introductory course for a beginner audience is quite different from one that provides advanced problem-solving or social skills.

Get as many people involved in the planning as you can. Ask for help from subject matter experts, managers, members, and instructors. The wider net you cast for members of the planning committee, the better your results. Delve into the profiles of your membership. What do they need? What are they asking for? What are their characteristics and demographics?

Talk to subject matter experts to gain information about the courses themselves. Can the material be broken into beginner, intermediate and advanced learners? Is there another logical break?

What do members need to know versus what is good to know? Remember that learners want relevant information that is useful to them and readily available when they need it. Nice-to-know information can make your courses long and reduce the perceived value to the members.

Take time to create a plan. It should be as detailed as necessary so that anyone who is new in the organization can look at it and understand what the next steps are. Make it a habit to never start an eLearning project without a plan or what might be called a Project Charter.

What should you do if you've already made this mistake? How do you fix it?

If you are like many Associations, you have courses you have already determined to be a candidate for eLearning or you have started development. If that is the case, here are a few steps to help you get on the right track for eLearning development.

First, step back and determine the direction and results you want to achieve with your eLearning program. This is a good time to check with members using a survey, conduct an interview with subject matter experts and create a high-level plan.

Then, analyze where your courses are now. What stage of development are they in? How far away from your goal? Look at the course objectives and content objectively to determine where you need to subtract or add information to reach your goal.

This is the time to make changes. Don't be afraid of change. It's easier to make them now than when your courses are rolled out to your members. Identify what changes need to be made right now.

Finally, develop a plan to implement the modifications. Take small steps and set realistic timelines for making the changes happen. Identify what help you need to get the results you want. Maybe it's time to hire a project manager with eLearning experience. Maybe you can do it in-house with some education. The important point is to implement!

How do we prevent making this mistake moving forward?

Preventing this mistake in the future begins with a commitment to never create an eLearning course without first developing a plan. It's best to look at least 1-2 years out while planning. You may not have all of the details, but you will have the basics which make the detailed planning easier.

A good way to help develop a plan is to make the eLearning development part of your budgeting process. This means that you have considered the needs of your members and have determined how much the eLearning components will cost. It also means that each year you will take a look at the eLearning plan in order to help develop the budget for the coming year.

It's always good to include a wide variety of people in your planning process. Some people to include are executives, members, subject matter experts, community resources, board members, and training staff/volunteers. When you involve others, the planning is more robust and you are more likely to successfully provide eLearning courses your members will appreciate.

Any tools or insight to help people get results faster, easier, more efficiently?

Any project management tools that you currently use to help develop a strategy will work fine. Here are some things to consider when working on your project plan.

1. Project Initiation. Discuss the following with the owner of the project.

- Project goals
- Course objectives
- Time lines
- Resources available
- Who is approving or signing-off on the project?
- Who is the final authority?

2. Resources. Assemble the group of people who will work on the project or who can provide information and feedback. Include a wide variety of people in the discussion. For example, association members, subject matter experts, IT resources, multimedia developers, etc.

3. Course Content. Identify the learner's and the association's needs. What does the organization want to do and what does the learner need to do? Use this information to build the content for the course.

4. Learning Strategy. Identify the methods you will use to present the information to the members. For example, does the information need to be presented in a linear fashion or using real-world scenarios. The strategy you choose will dictate how the course is programmed and presented.

5. Look and Feel. Use rapid development tools to create the look and feel for your course(s). Find a balance between sophistication and usability. Use templates, standard fonts, colors and images that convey the message you want the members to receive.

6. Multimedia. What media should you develop to include in your courses. Options include audio, video and flash resources. Decide who is going to create the components and how they will be used within the course.

7. Technical Issues. Identify where the course is going to be hosted and how the member will gain access to the course. Will the course be on a Learning Management System? Does it need to be AICC or SCORM compliant? What information do you need to track and how will you do it? What reports are needed? Bring your IT resource to the table early in the planning so you ask the right questions.

8. Training Roll Out & Evaluation. How will the members know the course is now available? What marketing do you need to do? How effective is the course? What improvements need to be made in the next edition? How will the course(s) be maintained?

Take all of this information and create a formal document that clearly spells out your plans and rationale. This document will help to guide the production and the evaluation of the course development process.

My BIGGEST piece of advice moving forward...

Planning is nothing without execution. Always take the time to plan your program before you begin developing the first course. Write it down and refer to it often. Revise the plan as you go along so that it meets the needs of your association.

Summary:

- Always strategize before getting started.
- Get as many people involved in developing the strategy as possible.
- Understand the purpose of the training before developing the first course.

- Write out the strategy in a formal document.
- Use the list of things to consider to verify your project plan is complete.

Mistake #2: My Staff Can Handle It.

What is the mistake?

Many associations make the mistake of thinking that their current training staff members will be able to develop an eLearning course easily. The thinking is that they are great stand-up trainers or subject matter experts so they should be able to create the course without any problems. Just because they are experienced trainers does not mean they are proficient in eLearning course development.

Your staff may spend a lot of time and energy developing what they think will be a great course only to discover that translating a standup course into eLearning is difficult. The learner can't ask questions and the trainer can't see when learners are confused or have questions.

Why it's a mistake

eLearning requires some specialized skills which are different than those for classroom training. eLearning also requires that the instructor be familiar with the technology and tools to implement the programs within the organization.

Often, the instructor does not know the best ways to translate current training and instruction into effective eLearning programs. It takes more than simply turning a PowerPoint Presentation into "instruction" online.

In associations, as with other organizations, the decision about selecting an eLearning platform is frequently made based upon financial resources rather than the needs of the students. The platform selected may not be the best for its intended use, and your current instructors are not always the best choice to make the determination.

Finally, the social aspect of the learner, self-motivation skills, and the student's confidence with technology will affect how well the student will prosper in an eLearning environment. Building in a social aspect in the courses requires additional technology skills that traditional classroom trainers are not accustomed to using.

What are the consequences of making this mistake and how critical are they?

The consequences of making this mistake are high. The association is wasting critical resources, both time and money, on a course that is not effective for your members. Your busy staff doesn't have the time to really learn what they need to be doing before taking on the project and will spend a lot of time learning about the technology and researching the various platforms.

Why and when do people tend to make this mistake?

This is a really common mistake that managers make. First of all, they assume that it's going to cost a lot of money to obtain outside assistance with their eLearning projects. But when you factor in all the learning curve, it can really be more cost effective to hire an experienced consultant to guide you in completing your first projects. Your staff can eventually figure it all out, but do you really want them to struggle with the programming aspect when help is easily available?

Another reason to obtain outside help is that your staff is not familiar with the technology and what it can do. If you only know the very basics of what the software can do, you will be missing out on the best functionality that can make your courses effective and fun to view. Your staff can read the books and take the expensive classes but without practical knowledge, they will still have difficulty with the process.

Getting assistance is not difficult. As I said before, local consultants at a smaller firm can be very cost effective in getting your programs up and running. Once your staff has experience in working with the software and the consultant, then it makes sense for them to begin to take over the course development.

Let me tell you a quick story to illustrate this point...

A retail client wanted to produce video training and put it on their Learning Management System for use by new hires and their current employees. They hired a production company to do the filming and editing but decided they could write their own scripts. The production company tried to talk them out of it because the client did not have any experience in developing content for video training. Their trainers had been doing a good job delivering the training in a classroom setting.

They spent thousands of dollars and the resulting videos were awful. The production values were great but the client used their own staff as talent with a script they wrote. The client eventually threw out all of the work and started from scratch using a professionally written video script with professional talent.

What should you do instead?

Take the time to understand the strengths and capabilities of your current staff. Identify any gaps in their knowledge or experience when it comes to eLearning. Some questions to ask include:

> "Do you have experience in writing scripts for eLearning courses?"
>
> "What media have you used in developing courses? Audio? Video? Computer-based Training (CBT)?"
>
> "Have you ever programmed a course using a professional eLearning software? If so, which one(s)?"
>
> "Are you experienced creating images using Adobe Photoshop, Adobe Illustrator or another graphic design program?

"Have you ever edited audio or video files? If so, what programs did you use?"

"Are you familiar with our Learning Management System (if you have one)? Or have they used a LMS previously? If so, which one?"

Consider the cost to have your staff learn the skills necessary to produce an eLearning course. This includes the time away from their current job as well as attending classes (online or in-person). If they don't have graphic design experience, what will it cost for you to obtain the pictures, illustrations, icons and images for your courses? Have they had experience in producing and editing audio or video? Do they have the equipment or will you need to purchase professional equipment and/or software?

Compare the resources required to implement your eLearning program with using a local expert. You may be pleasantly surprised. Even if the costs appear to be higher, be sure to consider the cost of rework or starting over a second time.

What should you do if you've already made this mistake? How do you fix it?

If you've already fallen in this trap, here's how you get out. Analyze where you are now. What skill gaps have you identified in your current staff? Where do you need additional assistance? Do you have an instructional design process that you are following? If not, be sure to identify a method to use in your project and implement it right now.

Focus on completing one course and get it done right. Don't be afraid to make changes to what you have already developed. Now is the time to go through the entire process using the appropriate tools to really understand where your staff needs assistance?

Take the time to plan out what needs to happen to get the course developed and implemented. Be sure you are not simply regurgitating pages of text pulled from book or classroom material. The final product should not be classroom instruction without the instructor. Build in appropriate interactions and identify ways for students to interact with other students and instructors. This social aspect is what helps make eLearning effective.

You may find that you will need a separate curriculum model for eLearning versus traditional classroom training. Perhaps you provide pre-work using the eLearning modules followed by classroom style interactions for questions and application.

How do we prevent making this mistake moving forward?

Find a consultant or eLearning development firm that you can work with and who works well with your staff. A good consultant will help to teach your staff how to work with the consulting firm to get the course developed at the lowest possible cost.

Know what is most important for your staff to be doing. Should they be developing the course content and acting as a subject matter expert or actually programming the course and designing graphics and multi-media elements?

There are different skill sets required for course development. The course designer works with the SME to gather and organize the content and write the scripts. Another person graphically creates the course and programs it. Most organizations try to combine these into one role. You may have a great programmer, but they may not understand how to develop the scripts. On the other hand, you may have a great designer, but they may not have the skills to program the course.

Any tools or insight to help people get results faster, easier, more efficiently?

The best model for eLearning instruction should include a method for creation and evaluation of material in the curriculum. The ideal model includes all four types of interaction and has a strong developmental stage that covers the complete process of designing curriculum from start to finish.

The Dick and Carey Model is a great model to use for eLearning. It progresses in a linear fashion and can incorporate all of the required design elements in a logical order.

The Four Levels of Interaction include:

1. Learner collaborates with other learners.
2. Learner receives content from instructional resources.
3. Learner receives guidance and mediation from instructor.
4. Learner uses technology easily to interface with content.

It's important in effective course development to include as many of these levels of interaction as possible in your course designs. For example, you might want to include a method of interaction with other students via a wiki or Private Google Group. Links to resources should be included with every module. The module could be the pre-requisite for a face-to-face or web conference where students receive guidance from the instructor. And finally, the ability to access the course content and move through the course easily while online (or offline if your LMS permits).

The order of design is also very important in the design hierarchy.

1. Technology should be considered first because of access issues and continual changes in resources. If technology is not the most up to date, a learner may have difficulty accessing all aspects of the learning environment. If technology is antiquated, the training may not be as interesting or interactive as necessary to provide the needed training.

2. Content must work with the technology and be appropriate for student learning. Since content changes fast in some fields, it must be examined from both the aspect of its use through e-technology and the learning that will take place.

3. Learner-to-learner interface. Learners must have multiple communication sources and be motivated to communicate among themselves. One of the most important aspects of learning is the sharing among peers. This aspect is often overlooked and should be an important part of the design process.

4. Instructor-learner interaction must be easy with immediate feedback. Without ease of communication and feedback in a timely manner, students become frustrated and disinterested in the process.

My BIGGEST piece of advice moving forward...

Doing it yourself does not always mean you will be cost effective, especially in the beginning as you ramp up your curriculum. Asking your current staff to take on the role of programmer and course developer can often cause frustration and dissatisfaction. Consider bringing in a consultant who will work with your staff to provide education and guidance throughout the eLearning program development.

Summary:

- Your staff may be great, but may not be the best choice to develop your eLearning programs.
- It's okay to use a consulting firm to help you get your courses developed.
- Work with the consultant to learn how to do it yourself the next time.
- Don't be like the client who insisted on doing it themselves, wasting time and energy after discovering the process needed major modification to redo the process.

Mistake #3: Being Agile Will Save The Day

What is the mistake?

The mistake that many managers make is to assume that simply using the latest "development method or software" will ensure their eLearning courses are well designed and effective for the audience. These methods come and go but sound Instructional Design will make the difference in your course effectiveness.

Why it's a mistake

Let's consider some of the reasons why this is a mistake. First of all, organizations don't implement the new process completely or understand the complexities and nuances of the new tool. They hear a little about something and read a couple of articles and think "That would work for us!" The manager then asks the design team to use the new tool or process without investigating whether it really will make a difference. Often requiring a new software tool simply confuses the process and slows everything down as people have to learn about it and then try to apply the process to what they are already doing.

Another reason this is a mistake is that the tools may not be appropriate for your organization. Most of us like to jump on the latest trend or upgrade to a new and better process or software. We often think that the latest and greatest tools are what we need to be using, even if you are a small organization. We tend to want to complicate everything. But in reality, simpler is better. Most of us don't use all of the features of any software package we own, so having the latest and greatest can be a waste of money.

What are the consequences of making this mistake and how critical are they?

The consequences of making this mistake can be high. Most associations do not have an abundance of money laying around that they can waste in delays, rework or software packages.

Think about the last time you had to learn a new process or how to use a new software package. What happened? Did you spend hours just trying to figure it out? Were you frustrated because the way you worked changed? Were you able to get your work done quickly and easily?

I'm not trying to say that using a different process or software package is necessarily a bad thing. In my experience, we don't spend the time or money to train people to use the process or software correctly and then wonder why people are frustrated and leave the organization.

Not everything new is right for every organization. It's important to evaluate and make sure what you are encouraging others to do or use is "right" for your organization and not just the latest "bright shiny object."

Why and when do people tend to make this mistake?

There are a number of reasons why Association Managers make this mistake. There is pressure from the executive board/team to produce training quickly and at a reasonable cost. There may be a push to reuse materials and not always be in "development" mode. The subject matter experts feel pressure to share their knowledge without really understanding how the eLearning process works. Your members are asking for training quickly and you don't have a lot of resources available to complete the project.

You may be working with a consultant who is pushing you to use a specific method or software program because they have experience with it or receive some compensation for recommending it.

And because you are an association manager and not an instructional designer, you may not have enough information to evaluate a new system or process. You are relying upon others to help you make that decision.

And finally, maybe you have read about the new method and the sales materials that come with it and think the new product or process sounds really great. It's new and shiny and you want it.

Let me tell you a quick story to illustrate this point...

I work with 2 smaller production companies that have been around for 20+ years. They both are great at what they do.

Company A promotes video training. That's it. They know how to write scripts and provide a great training experience if what you want is video training.

Company B promotes themselves as an eLearning company. However, this company believes that every course needs to have a video component in it. No matter what! They also promote using only one type of LMS system and development software for their courses.

Now, if you were to listen to each of their sales pitches, you would be convinced you need their services. But they may not be what you need for your organization.

Professional video production is expensive and difficult to update. Being tied to a specific software for your LMS limits the choices that may be more appropriate to your situation. Creating courses in only one software package can also limit who works on your production and may be more costly.

What should you do instead?

So what does the Association Manager need to do to develop training materials and send them out to the members in a way that makes sense to the organization?

First of all, don't fall for the latest training trend unless you have done your homework. Just because something is new does not mean it is better or appropriate for your members. For example, if you understand that your members are new to eLearning, you won't want to include a lot of technology that relies on their smartphone to answer or ask questions. They may not even have a smartphone!

Next, make sure you perform a thorough analysis of your members as it relates to eLearning. This is somewhat different than an analysis for learning in general. You will want to understand what their experience with eLearning is. How they access the training content. If they are comfortable with online learning in general. If they require documentation that they passed the course using some kind of assessment.

Understanding what the learner's experience with eLearning is will help you determine the type of eLearning course you need to develop, the development model to use and the type of software best suited to your Associations' needs.

Once you have a greater understanding of your members' eLearning experience and requirements, pick a development model you are comfortable using. Use it a few times to make sure you understand all of the components. Only then make modifications to fit your organization's needs.

What should you do if you've already made this mistake? How do you fix it?

If you've already fallen in this trap, here's how you get out. Take a step back and analyze your current development process. Determine how far off it is from where you want to be. Ask yourself if you are using a specific methodology or are making it up as you go along.

Determine the changes you need to make in your process to get where you want to go. This can be difficult because making changes in a program that is well underway may seem like the wrong thing to do. Keep in mind that if you are experiencing problems now, ignoring them rather than fixing them now is a big mistake. Don't be afraid to make needed changes.

If you are unsure, consult with an expert instructional designer. An experienced instructional designer should be able to work with your team and make recommendations for proceeding in the future. Don't be afraid to ask for advice and support.

How do we prevent making this mistake moving forward?

Be sure to follow a sound Instructional Design model when planning your eLearning courses. Choose one model or develop your own system and stick with it. Don't take shortcuts when using a particular model or procedure. Follow the steps to ensure you are including everything you need.

Make sure you have completed the needs analysis upfront so you really understand what your members want to get out of the eLearning course. Your members probably expect different outcomes from an online course than from a facilitated session so make sure you understand what those differences are.

Be careful using an AGILE model because it's easy to keep modifying and changing things and never actually finish the module.

Any tools or insight to help people get results faster, easier, more efficiently?

I prefer a method that takes a systems approach to Instructional Design. It's also known as the Dick and Carey Model. With this model, the components are executed iteratively and in parallel rather than following a linear process.

The model starts with **identifying Instructional Goals**. The goal statement describes the skill, knowledge or attitude (SKA) that you expect the learner to acquire. This is a critical step to ensure that your members are getting effective training that meets their needs.

Next you would **conduct an Instructional Analysis**. This is where you identify what the learner will need to know or do as a result of the instructions. For example: What must a learner be able to recall? What steps must the learner be able to do to complete a particular task? Asking these questions upfront will help to ensure the course meets the specific requirements for success.

You should also **Analyze Learners and Contexts**. This means that you will identify the general characteristics of the learners including what they already know, their prior experience with the content, basic demographics of the learners and any characteristics that are directly related to the knowledge, skill or behavior being taught.

With the information you have gathered to this point, you are ready to **write the Performance Objectives**. This is a description of the behavior, the condition and the criteria for performance. This is how you will decide if the learner has the knowledge, skills and abilities to perform the task or behavior being taught.

With the Performance Objectives in place, you can now **develop the Assessment Instruments**. This testing should have a purpose behind each question. Why are you testing? Is there a Pre-Test? Is there a Post-Test? What level of performance will be required? In some cases, a Pre- and Post- test are necessary for compliance purposes. In other cases, testing is not relevant to the performance. The skills will be demonstrated in a different manner other than paper and pencil or online testing.

At this point you are ready to **develop your Instructional Strategy**. This is where you decide if there are to be any activities that must be done in advance of the training. Determine the content to be presented, how the learners will participate (in class, online, blended), and what assessment will be required. This is also where you take a look at your technology to decide what platforms and software your organization can support.

Gather, develop and select the Instructional Materials to be used in the course. Do you have instructional materials that were used in previous courses? Are there PowerPoint Presentations available? Software manuals or instructional guides? This is where most instructional development begins and ends. As you can see from the model, this step should only occur after you have done a considerable amount of analysis.

This next step and those that follow are often omitted from the development process. Once the course is developed, it's important to **conduct a Formative Evaluation** of the Instruction. The formative evaluation is usually conducted during the development or early in the implementation process to obtain information about how to improve the course. Based on the recommendation from the Formative Evaluation, the course materials would be revised and improved. This would include making changes to the content, method of delivery, graphic designs, or assessments.

The final step before rollout is to **conduct the Summative Evaluation**. A summative evaluation is used at the end of the design process to determine whether a program should be adopted, continued, or modified for improvement.

Let's take a look at a couple of other popular development models and some of their weaknesses.

ADDIE is an instructional design method which consists of five phases: Analysis, Design, Development, Implementation and Evaluation. This model has been used as a guideline for building effective training programs. In this model, each step is completed and the information then feeds into the next step of the process.

Analysis Phase. In this phase the team asks questions about the problem, the audience, the purpose of the instruction and any constraints that are present. This is important information that then feeds into the Design considerations.

Design Phase. The recommendation for the Design phase is to use a systematic and logical method of identifying, developing and evaluating the planned strategies to reach the project's goals. This design phase requires a lot of attention to detail as the team considers the learning objectives, assessment tools, subject matter analysis, content, lesson planning and media selection. This is the phase where outlines and storyboards are created and approved.

Development Phase. This is where the content is translated into the programming. The programmers develop the content in the appropriate software, insert the multi-media and test the resulting course. The programmers debug the program and make any changes needed based upon the feedback from pilot users.

Implementation Phase. Now that the course is programmed, it's time to train the facilitators about the course curriculum, learning outcomes, delivery method, and testing procedures. This may mean preparing the learners to use eLearning tools and registering for the courses. This is also where the project manager makes sure that materials are ready, the software is in place and that the users can access the course online.

Evaluation Phase. This phase is a little tricky. Evaluation happens throughout the process in each stage of the model. At the end, an evaluation of the functionality and criteria for success is evaluated, often using the feedback of the students.

This is a great process but it is not without its weaknesses. For example, each of the phases requires a lot of upfront analysis which does not happen in most organizations. The teams simply don't have the time or the resources to perform the required level of analysis.

Another weakness is that the rigid design process makes creativity more difficult. There is very little accommodation for dealing with creative ideas or faults in the content.

There are many variations of this model available. Each was developed to get around the weaknesses in the system.

AGILE OR RAPID PROTOTYING developed out of the ADDIE model. This is the idea of receiving continual feedback during the instructional development phases. It is designed to catch and fix problems while they are still easy to correct. Using this method, there is overlap in the processes. For example, the needs analysis and content are revised based upon the knowledge that is gained by actually building and using the course.

This method is also not without its pitfalls. For example, rapid prototyping can cost a lot more money as you risk developing a course that is rejected and the work that was completed is discarded.

It does, however, promote better understanding of what the final eLearning course will look like since the elements are being developed at the same time as the content.

Another downside is that the prototype phase may never end and the course may never be delivered. This can affect all of the future course development as well. It's going to make it harder to do the upfront analysis that is necessary for good course design, especially for courses that do not have static content or those that are designed to change behavior.

My BIGGEST piece of advice moving forward...

Choose one method of instructional design and follow it through to completion. Don't jump around and use bits of one program and bits of another. The method of delivery is not as important as determining the audience needs and then developing a program to address those needs. Be careful using an AGILE or Rapid Prototyping methodology as it's easy to get caught continually fixing the program without ever actually launching the training.

Summary:

- Don't fall for the latest trend in instructional design.
- It's ok to modify a model, but use it carefully.
- Make sure you go through all of the analysis phase before you choose a method.
- The Dick and Carey model can be very effective.

Mistake #4: Let's Program This Course More Than Once

What is the mistake?

The mistake here is not taking the time to develop the course plans, outlines, or storyboards and jumping right into programming the course. This is a mistake because you will often end up throwing out all the work you have started when you discover that the course is not flowing in an acceptable manner. Sometimes you have the wrong information or too much information for the course you are developing.

Why it's a mistake

People make this mistake because they feel rushed to get the project done. Or maybe they think that just because they have content from the subject matter expert or a previous course, they don't need to spend time creating an outline and storyboard. That's a big mistake.

Association Managers often rely upon SMEs to provide the content for their members. Maybe it was a presentation at a conference or a paper written for publication. Translating these trainings into content that makes sense and provides value to your members will require some planning and preparation. Very rarely will you receive training information that will easily translate into an online course.

What are the consequences of making this mistake?

The consequences of making this mistake can be high. Not only will you spend time reworking the content after the course is programmed, but it will cost you money to do so.

You also risk providing disjointed content or too much content for the audience. If you have received documentation from a subject matter expert, chances are the material can be broken down into several levels for the audience: Beginner, Intermediate and Advanced content. Trying to put all of the information into one course means the course is too long and does not meet the needs of your members.

Without a plan, your course is doomed from the start. You risk developing a module or series of modules that do not flow well and provides more information than can be consumed in one sitting. Learners need for the information to be what they need, when they need it, and in small segments. Remember that an online course can provide a lot of information in 20 minutes, more than what can be provided in a classroom setting.

Why and when do people tend to make this mistake?

There are many reasons why Association Managers make this mistake. You are relying upon the subject matter expert to provide the information or even be in charge of the training development. They may be experts in their field but unfamiliar with the requirements for developing good eLearning courses.

The material provided by the SME does not translate easily into an online learning program. I find that most experts put too much information on each of their PowerPoint slides. They don't discriminate about the content because they know so much about the topic and are excited about it. They don't realize they are overwhelming their audience with too much material. It's important to identify the "need to know" versus the "nice to know" information before programming the course.

Many times you are rushed to get the training program out to your members and don't take the time to plan carefully. Planning can really benefit your eLearning programs. Be sure to take the time, up front, to plan. Even spending a few minutes or a couple of hours can save you time, money and frustration as you work through the programming process.

And finally, your instructional design team may not have the experience working with eLearning development and software to be effective.

Let me tell you a quick story to illustrate this point...

Recently I took over a project from an organization that was trying to do the course development in-house. They thought they would save a lot of money because their subject matter experts or

SMEs had been providing the training and it would be easy to just put it into an online format. They would be good to go!

Unfortunately for the company, the inexperienced team created a program that was way too long and overly complicated for the audience. They were relying upon the PowerPoint slides the SMEs used to create the training. If they had asked, they would have found out that the training the SMEs were providing was not well received and everyone dreaded sitting through another boring PowerPoint presentation.

After careful analysis, we broke the long and complicated course into multiple modules that made logical sense and flowed smoothly from one to another. The 90 minute training program became four 15-20 minute modules with quizzes and knowledge checks that helped the learner's comprehension and application on the job.

What should you do instead?

Planning should not be the end result. It should lead you through the development process in a way that allows you to provide value to your members. Ultimately, creating a plan will save you time and money.

The first step is to identify the end user for your training. Are the members new to this topic or very experienced? Their level of knowledge will help to guide the rest of this process. For example, if you are creating a course for a newbie, you would want to ensure that you provide the background for the topic: why it's important and why they should care.

If it's a course for experienced learners you can omit some of the background information and get straight to a burning issue or critical question. The way the course is designed will be different in each situation.

The second step is to ask your members what it is they want to know. It's easy to create surveys using online tools or even by sending a simple email.

Next, consider the information you have gathered and create an outline. The outline can be as simple or as complicated as you wish. Many times I find that it's easier to create a very detailed outline that I can share with the subject matter experts for their feedback. By providing talking points and sometimes the actual words I will use in the course narration, the rest of the process goes much more quickly. The SME's have information to use to provide feedback and I know where there are gaps in information.

After the SMEs have reviewed the outlines, it much easier to create a storyboard. I generally use PowerPoint to create the storyboard for several reasons. The most important reason is that PowerPoint is a program that most people use and understand. When creating the storyboard, I use the slide to show the on-screen bullets and images or simply text boxes with descriptions of the interactions that I have planned. I use the notes section at the bottom of each slide to write the script for the narrator if there is one.

Once again, I provide the SMEs or other approvers the opportunity to suggest changes. All of this happens before the first screen is programmed. Fortunately for us, many of the software programs used to create the eLearning courses can import PowerPoint slides directly into the software so creating the storyboard doesn't waste time—it actually saves it!

What should you do if you've already made this mistake? How do you fix it?

If you've already made this mistake here are some things you can do to remedy the situation. First, take a look at the information you have gathered from the SME. Where are the gaps? How can you break the information down to meet your member's needs? Identify the material that should be provided to each level: Beginner, Intermediate and Advanced.

Now arrange the information into logical chunks in an outline. You can even create one long outline that you can break down into modules later. The point is to get the information to flow smoothly from beginning to end.

Share the outline with the SMEs and get their feedback. We will talk more about this step later in this document. The important point is to make sure that when you consolidate and reduce the content you are still providing accurate information to the members.

Work with an Instructional Designer to identify what needs to be changed and if there is any content that can be reused. Again, don't be afraid to make changes now. If you put out a course that is too long and convoluted, you will lose your audience for future modules. Do the best you can with your very first module and get the process and content right.

How do we prevent making this mistake moving forward?

So what can you do to prevent this issue from happening again? No matter what course you are creating, whether it's from scratch or from a previous course, take the time to do some planning before you get too far into development. Follow these steps:

1. Identify your audience for the course.
2. Answer the question: "What do the learners need to know or do?"
3. Create an outline and share it with the SME's for feedback.
4. Develop the storyboard from the reviewed outline and share with approvers for feedback.

5. Share your approved storyboard with the course programmer.

Don't rely solely on the SME for direction. Share the outline with others for their feedback. Consider sharing the outline with new and experienced members and any training staff you have. I have even shared basic content with people outside the field to identify any gaps in the information. This is a great way to identify jargon and acronyms that need defined.

Evaluate the current course content and include the resulting analysis into future module development. Consider the lessons learned from the initial courses you developed and include them in your planning process.

Never create a module without planning first.

Any tools or insight to help people get results faster, easier, more efficiently?

Keep it simple. I use Microsoft Word to create my outlines. Outlines for eLearning can be less formal than an outlines you used to use to create a white paper or formal document. Typically I use the title of the slide and then use bullet points to develop the content.

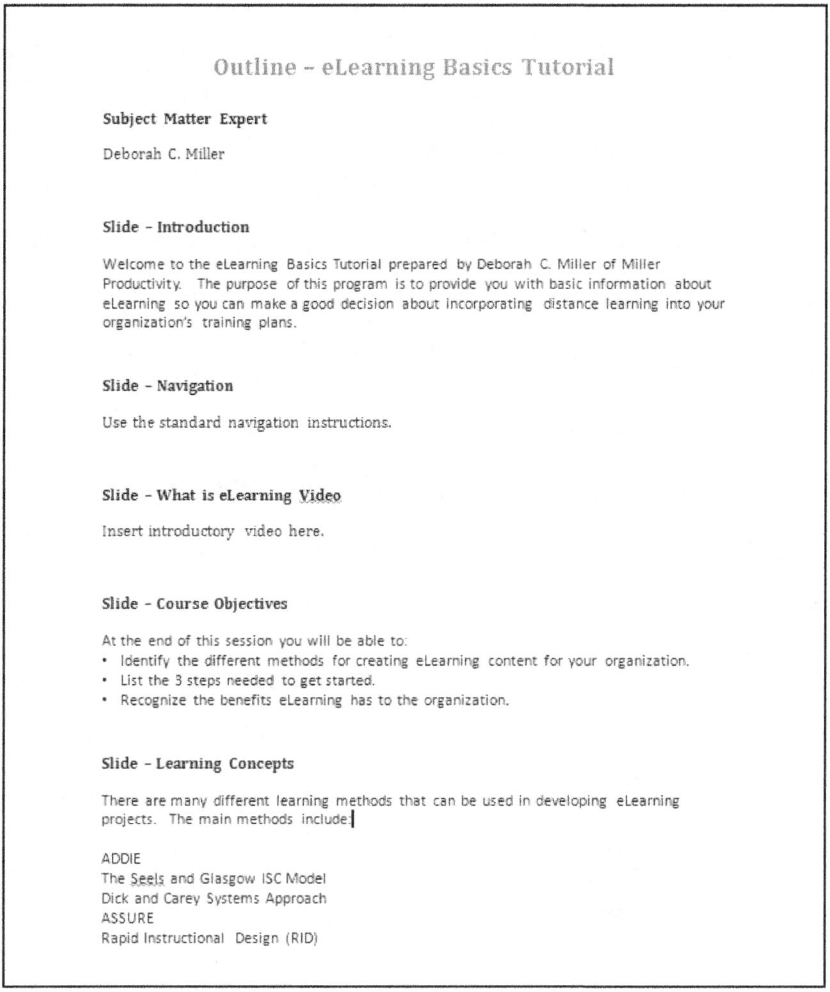

Outline – eLearning Basics Tutorial

Subject Matter Expert

Deborah C. Miller

Slide – Introduction

Welcome to the eLearning Basics Tutorial prepared by Deborah C. Miller of Miller Productivity. The purpose of this program is to provide you with basic information about eLearning so you can make a good decision about incorporating distance learning into your organization's training plans.

Slide – Navigation

Use the standard navigation instructions.

Slide – What is eLearning Video

Insert introductory video here.

Slide – Course Objectives

At the end of this session you will be able to:
- Identify the different methods for creating eLearning content for your organization.
- List the 3 steps needed to get started.
- Recognize the benefits eLearning has to the organization.

Slide – Learning Concepts

There are many different learning methods that can be used in developing eLearning projects. The main methods include:

ADDIE
The Seels and Glasgow ISC Model
Dick and Carey Systems Approach
ASSURE
Rapid Instructional Design (RID)

I never try to use the traditional outline hierarchy when creating outlines for eLearning. I do indent bullets when the content is complicated and needs an additional level. Some software programs do not import bullets well. For example, Storyline only accepts one level of bullet points, so I try to minimize how often they are used.

Once you have received all of the recommended changes from the SMEs, copy and paste the information from your outline into PowerPoint to create the storyboard.

Each PowerPoint slide represents a page in the course module. Be sure to put your programming notes and images on the slide itself. I use colored text boxes to identify notes to the programmer, interaction suggestions, and questions for the SME.

There is a feature in PowerPoint that allows you to save an image of the slide with the notes next to the slide in a table. This makes it easy for reviewers to make changes. Go to **File→Export** and choose **Create Handouts.**

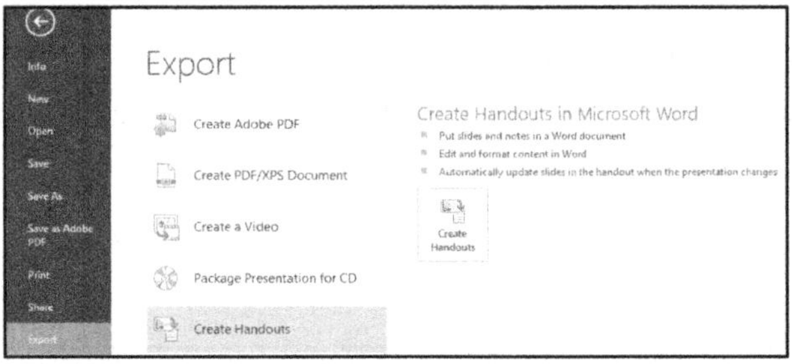

Note: Your screen may look different depending upon the version of PowerPoint you are using but the functionality is the same.

Click **Create Handouts** to open the layout selections.

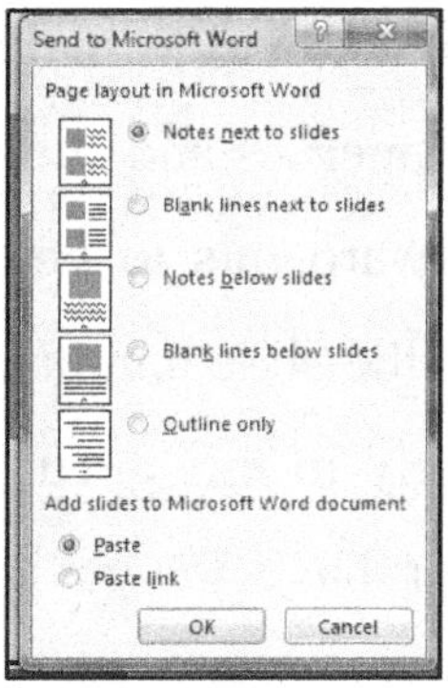

I select to print the Notes next to the slides and Paste the slides into the document.

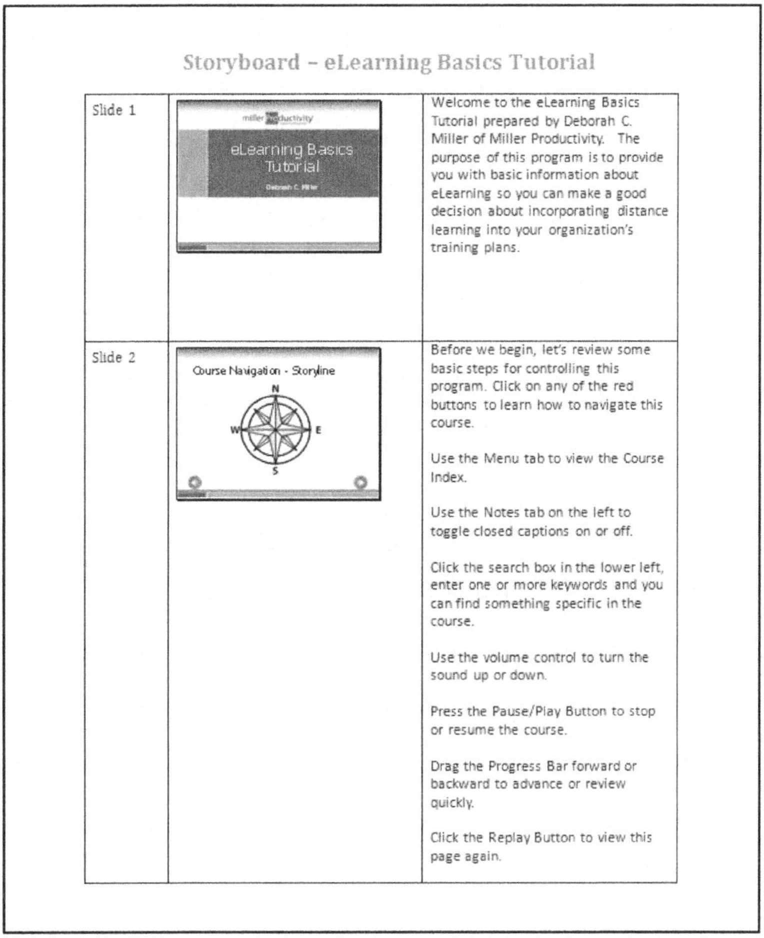

Storyboard – eLearning Basics Tutorial

Slide 1	miller productivity eLearning Basics Tutorial Deborah C. Miller	Welcome to the eLearning Basics Tutorial prepared by Deborah C. Miller of Miller Productivity. The purpose of this program is to provide you with basic information about eLearning so you can make a good decision about incorporating distance learning into your organization's training plans.
Slide 2	Course Navigation - Storyline N W E S	Before we begin, let's review some basic steps for controlling this program. Click on any of the red buttons to learn how to navigate this course. Use the Menu tab to view the Course Index. Use the Notes tab on the left to toggle closed captions on or off. Click the search box in the lower left, enter one or more keywords and you can find something specific in the course. Use the volume control to turn the sound up or down. Press the Pause/Play Button to stop or resume the course. Drag the Progress Bar forward or backward to advance or review quickly. Click the Replay Button to view this page again.

Open the document and format the header and footer text. I also open the Table Properties and show "All" of the borders. Save the document and forward this to your Subject Matter Experts to review. They can see the slide annotation as well as the text which they can change directly in this document. I also turn on Review and Track Changes or have the reviewer highlight changes they make.

My BIGGEST piece of advice moving forward...

My best advice? Keep it simple. Use the tools you already know and that are widely available to everyone in the organization. Just be sure to complete the planning process before you begin to program the course.

Summary:

- Always create an outline and storyboard and have it reviewed by the Subject Matter Experts before you begin to program any course.
- Don't let your course designer start programming before you have solidified the content.
- Use the tools you know to create the outline and storyboard for each course.
- Keep it simple.

Mistake #5: Look What I Designed!

What is the mistake?

Another mistake that is made is not developing a design plan and style sheet for your eLearning projects. The result of this mistake is that the design becomes an afterthought and your projects will not have a cohesive look and feel. In addition, your projects lose the professionalism that your members expect.

Why it's a mistake

Design documents are created during the initial design phase of the instructional design process. The document provides all of the necessary information about the course to your design team. This includes the instructional designers, graphic artists, multimedia specialists, programmers, project manager, writers and anyone else who is involved in the project. If you have multiple programmers or a number of courses to develop, not having a style sheet will result in courses that look and function differently. You lose any branding opportunities that set your association apart.

What are the consequences of making this mistake and how critical are they?

The information included in the design documents will depend upon the project itself and the course requirements. If you are doing a series of eLearning courses, this document becomes crucial as you develop a cohesive theme or look and feel.

In addition, there are differences in the skill levels of the programmers working on your modules. Some programmers are also adept at using graphic software such as Illustrator or Photoshop to create stunning graphics. Others are not quite as talented.

By not defining the standards upfront, you will lose your ability to specify the look and feel of the project and the resulting final course. If you are unhappy with the result, the designer can come back and say that you didn't specify the graphical elements and may be unwilling to make changes without suitable compensation.

It also helps at the start of the process to identify the programmers and graphic artists you will need to have working on your project. You will know what skill level you need to hire. For example, if you don't need a lot of graphics then someone with less skill in that area may be fine and will often cost you less. A person with better graphical skills will probably be more expensive. You want to hire for the skill level you need.

Why and when do people tend to make this mistake?

This mistake is very common, especially for inexperienced developers. If you don't know what to specify, you might leave it up to the programmer to decide. Sometime that works out great. Other times, not so much. A good programmer will ask questions to determine what look and feel you are expecting. If you leave it up to the programmer you are taking a chance.

Let me tell you a quick story to illustrate this point...

I am currently involved in developing a series of training modules for an educational facility. We have identified 19 modules that need to be created within a short period of time. This means that we will have multiple people developing the storyboards and programming the final courses.

Since I'm writing the outlines and interviewing the Subject Matter Experts, I created a template so that my outlines are consistent and include the same information. For example, I always include the names of the Subject Matter Experts that I interviewed at the top of the document. Recommended resources and potential video elements are included at the end of the outline. This makes it easier later on when we are developing the Resource links and filming the videos for each module. I also know who needs to review and approve the final outline.

Determining the voice of the project is also important. Will you use first or second person? Being consistent throughout in your outlines and storyboards will be important. Another question that comes up is how to capitalize and spell some words. For example, is it e-learning, elearning, or eLearning? Consistency is critical to a professional-looking course.

I also needed to establish the module naming convention. This might seem like a small thing, but when you start having a number of people working on the same course, how you name the files will be important.

I'm an Instructional Designer, not a graphic artist. I understand how to develop the course using good instructional design methods and adult learning theories. Graphic designers understand how the elements should go together on the page so it looks great. These two roles must work together in order to develop a course that is effective and incorporates the proper level of interactivity and graphic elements.

Going back to my educational course example, the graphic designer played a key role in developing the look and feel for the course. It's a great temptation to think that the Instructional Designer can also play the role of graphic designer to save money. Don't do it. Your Instructional Designer should provide direction to the Graphic Designer. But not spending the time and money up front to come up with the graphic elements is a huge mistake. Graphic Designers are creative people who like to put their own spin on projects. If you have multiple designers involved, your projects will look disjointed. Even when there is a style sheet, you may find that the Designers interpret the ideas just a little bit differently. Using a single Graphic Designer can help alleviate this problem.

What should you do instead?

Get a graphic designer involved from the very beginning of the project to help establish the design requirements. Then work with your team to develop the conventions you will use to create the design documents for the project. Create and distribute a style sheet to everyone on the team and stick to it! It will be a temptation to make changes to individual modules because you are bored with the design. Again, don't do it. Assign a reviewer to ensure that the style sheet is being used in every module you develop.

What should you do if you've already made this mistake? How do you fix it?

If you've already developed an eLearning module or two, take some time to review each course and determine what you like and don't like about the design. What design elements just don't work for you? Is the font easy to read or is it too small on the screen or scrunched together? What about the colors? Are they the same in each course or do they look totally different.

Next decide what elements you want to use going forward and start to create your Style Sheet. It may not be practical to go back and recreate your modules, but you can make the decision going forward to standardize your design.

How do we prevent making this mistake moving forward?

It's simple—never create an eLearning module without developing a Style Sheet or using one you currently have. It is important from a branding standpoint that your courses look and feel the same for the user. Your members will come to expect the same quality for all of the modules you offer and when the look and feel is the same, the audience will be more comfortable and like them more.

It can be difficult to get the graphic designers to buy-in to your plan, but be persistent. If the graphic designer was involved from the beginning in making the decisions, they will more likely follow the Style Sheet criteria. It's your course, and you have to make sure everyone from the writer, to the graphic designer, to the programmer all know what the criteria is and that they follow it.

Any tools or insight to help people get results faster, easier, more efficiently?

The Style Sheet can be a living document and includes information as it becomes available. Here are some things to add to your Style Sheet document:

Background Information: This includes the reasons for developing the training, the course objectives, major topics and the overall goals for your training program.

Project Scope: This is a brief statement that outlines what will be included and what NOT to include in your course development.

Target Audience: This is based on your needs analysis and the overall goals of the project. For example, if you are writing to a beginner audience your information will be very different than if you are writing for an experienced audience. Know your audience. I recommend defining the characteristics of your audience and personalizing the information. Give your target Association Member a name. Describe them. Then when you are writing the content, you can write to a single individual to make the content more meaningful to your audience.

Prerequisites: Do your courses need to be taken in a particular order? Does the Target Audience need to have specific knowledge before they take the course? Be sure to identify any prerequisites and include that information in the document.

Graphic Design: How will the learners move through your course (the navigation)? What style of images will you include (vector graphics, illustrations or photos)? What colors will be used (CMYK, RGB)? How will the information be displayed on the screen (bullet points, scroll bars, images, text)? What is the look and feel? What will the buttons and links look like? Where will they be located on the screen? Will you use a tabular format or icons? What will the icons look like?

Media Elements: Will there be video? Animations? Narration? Other Audio components? Describe the proposed elements and include any budget restrictions. Who will provide the media elements (SME, course developer, outside resource)?

Interactions: Will you require the learner to interact with the content? How will that be accomplished (click, drag and drop, knowledge checks, ungraded quizzes, role plays, case studies)?

Voice: Will you use first person? Second person? How will you present case studies, role plays, exercises? Singular or plural?

Delivery Methods: How will the course be delivered (online, classroom, blended)? If online, how will the learners access the content?

Course Outlines/Storyboards: How will you structure the course? Will you include screen shots in the outlines or only in the storyboard? What content will be included (videos, text, examples, case studies)? Who will provide the content? What format will you use to create these documents? Microsoft Word? PowerPoint? Storyline? Other? Do you have a template? Do you have written instructions for how to create the document for review?

Evaluation Strategy: Will learners be required to pass a test upon course completion? How will that be managed (within the course or external testing)? Have you considered how to track ROI (Return on Investment)? Will learners receive CEUs (Continuing Education Units)? How will that be managed?

Development Tools: Do the courses need to be developed using a specific software (PowerPoint, Storyline, Camtasia, Photoshop, and Illustrator)? Does the development tool make sense for the project? If not, what recommendations do you have for the development process?

Technical Requirements: What operating system will you need to plan for? Where will the content be stored? What plugins or players will be used? Are there memory restrictions? What platform will be used to deliver the content (Moodle, Articulate Online, or Cloud Storage)? What other requirements must be considered?

Compliance Requirements: Do the courses have to meet SCORM or Section 508 requirements?

Project Management: Who will be the project manager? Where will the timeline and project documents be located (Google, Cloud Sharing, SharePoint, other)? Who will track and maintain project sign-off names and contact information? Who is responsible for project reviews and quality assurance?

My BIGGEST piece of advice moving forward...

My best advice to you is to plan your courses well from the very beginning. If you take the time to create a Style Sheet and planning documents upfront, the rest of the project will proceed much more smoothly. Use a shared location to store the documents. I really like using Google Drive because the documents are available to anyone from any computer. People can work in the documents together. It doesn't matter what system everyone is using, MAC or PC. Your graphic designer can be on an Apple computer and you can be on a PC. The files work for all.

Summary:

- Take the time to create a style sheet and requirements before you begin.
- Use the Style Sheet to maintain consistency throughout your courses.

Mistake #6: Let's Make The User Click Again

What is the mistake?

Instructional Designers are told by the client to make the content "interactive" so the learner doesn't get bored. What happens then, is that the Designer and Programmer add an interaction just because they can and have been directed to do so without thought as to why you are including that interaction at all. They often rely upon the same old tired interactions they always use—click on an icon or button to view more information.

Why it's a mistake

This is a mistake for a couple of reasons. Learners need a reason to engage with the content. They have a wide variety of experience that they bring to the learning situation. If you just have them click on every page, you aren't engaging them with the content. It's like turning a page—you do it because you have to get to the next bit of content. That is not engagement.

Another reason it's a mistake is that there are many ways to engage your learners using eLearning methods. Many of these methods don't require a lot of programming skill on your part. They simply require you to be creative and think about the learner's experience.

Developers make this mistake because adding interactions can be time consuming and require additional programming support.

You may need to include additional time and resources to your projects for complicated interactions. It's much easier to create a page-turning script than to write branching scenarios. The branching scenarios can be more effective if done well, but they also take a lot more time to write and develop.

What are the consequences of making this mistake and how critical are they?

The consequences of making this mistake are high. You risk losing the attention of the learner as they proceed through the course. They may question how much it cost them to take the course as opposed to buying a book that they can page through. They could be unwilling to purchase another course from the Association because of their experience with the first one.

The content needs to be developed in a way that makes the learner say "Wow! That was a great experience, let me take another course."

Why and when do people tend to make this mistake?

An inexperienced Instructional Designer or Writer will often make this mistake, especially if they are not familiar with the software that is being used to create the eLearning module. If they are only familiar with creating modules using PowerPoint, for example, they may not know how to develop a course using

Articulate or Storyline. The interactions available in PowerPoint are very different than what you can do in an eLearning software.

The budget is another reason people make this mistake. It does cost more to develop an eLearning module that includes different interactions than just creating a PowerPoint show. The Association may not have the budget to hire an experienced instructional designer or programmer. It's better to spend the time and money to develop one amazing course than to offer many that don't meet the needs of the learner. You can often use the elements of the first module to build the next ones.

Another reason for this mistake is time restraints. You may need to have the module ready in a short period of time for an important launch. It takes time to develop the interactions and to test them with your audience. Sometimes it's just better to get a course out there and worry about adding interactions later.

And finally, programmer inexperience can be a factor. If you are using a programmer with limited experience, it may take them a long time to figure out what needs to be done to make the more complicated interactions work.

Let me tell you a quick story to illustrate this point...

An organization I work with hired an experienced videographer to come to work with the organization to program

Storyline courses. He is really great at creating awesome videos but didn't know anything about creating a course in the software.

The Instructional Designer created a module with a lot of interactions from a main page. It was a map where the user would click on each building to learn more about the organization. This required a programmer with lots of experience, which he did not have. He gave it a valiant effort, but ultimately the project became behind schedule and another programmer had to rescue the project.

The programmer was able to create simple interactions that used templates for quizzes and page turning. But he was unable to do anything that was complicated.

What should you do instead?

It's important to understand the learner's needs and expectations. A short course may not require much more than a few basic interactions. However, if the content lends itself to branching or multiple paths, be sure to hire an experienced programmer who knows the software you use.

If you are planning to create the courses in-house, it pays to send your most experienced team members to training. This should include not only the instructional designer, but the graphic designer and the programmer. That way, everyone knows what the software can do and the complexity level of the interactions.

What should you do if you've already made this mistake? How do you fix it?

Depending upon how the course was created, it may make sense to go back to each module and think about how to add an interaction to make the course more interesting and engaging to the learner.

Determine where you can add an interaction to check the learner's knowledge since that is an easy way to engage the learner in the content. Or maybe add a scenario that asks the learner "What would you do?" Have the user type their answer and view the recommended response. If you haven't done so, add a quiz at the end. It can be graded or ungraded.

How do we prevent making this mistake moving forward?

Begin to think about an interaction as something that mentally engages the learner…not just "stuff" they can click on or do for the sake of clicking or doing. As part of your Style Sheet, identify some criteria for adding interactions in your courses.

Perhaps every module should have a video or knowledge check. If a scenario makes sense, think about how to write one that fits with their everyday experience.

Investigate the many interactions that are available within your chosen software so you know what is possible. Then pick one to try. Don't try to include too many interactions in a module. Remember the module should only take 20-30 minutes to complete so adding one or two interactions could be enough.

Any tools or insight to help people get results faster, easier, more efficiently?

Here are some simple and effective interactions you can add to your courses to engage the learner and make the content more interesting.

Scenarios. A scenario can be added as a stand-alone item within the training or they can be used to guide the entire course. There are 3 main types of scenarios that are frequently used in eLearning courses.

"What Would You Do?" Scenarios. To use this scenario within your course, simply provide a paragraph of text or an image to provide the context for the scenario. Then ask the question, "What would you do?" Leave a blank field for the learners to type in their response to the question. Then you provide a suggested response once they have submitted their response. This allows the learner to compare their answer with the suggested response. This is a simple and effective way to provide an interaction that does not require fancy graphics or programmer.

As an illustration, the educational courses I am working on, have a number of scenarios that a teacher would encounter. For each situation, we prepared a suggested response and the rationale for why that response is more correct. The teachers can then see how well the learners have absorbed the material presented earlier in the course as they apply what they have learned to situations they will likely encounter.

Multiple Choice Scenarios. For this type of scenario, you would provide the context in written text or an image on the screen. Then ask a question about that scenario and provide several potential answers for the learner to select. The easiest way to use this method is to plan for learners to answer the question correctly. If they don't answer correctly, provide them with the correct answer and the rationale for the response. It is possible to provide a link back to the earlier information within the course. Using multiple choice responses also allows you to collect data about the question. For example, if everyone is missing the same question, you might want to consider modifying the content within the course to be clearer.

Branching Scenarios. This method provides a great opportunity for students to learn from their mistakes. You would let the learner go down the wrong path for some period of time to see where it gets them. This is a way to provide a realistic range of possibilities and consequences.

The key to creating successful branching scenarios is to limit most branches to 2 choices to help limit the complexity of the programming. The trick is to control the length of your scenario as you go along so you are within the scope of the project.

Questions & Answers. Questions and Answers are often included in eLearning courses. We use them as pre- or post-testing, and for knowledge checks. Using the pre/post-tests allows you to see if there is improvement in knowledge or understanding of the content being presented. It also helps you to understand where your student's are in terms of the content before they take the course. If the majority of your learners can pass the pre-test, your content may need to be adjusted to provide advanced material.

A feature of eLearning software that is not used very often is a progress meter. Instead of just tracking how much of the quiz or course is complete, think about unique ways you can use to incorporate a meter in your courses. For example, have the learner answer customer questions and their overall sales increase or decrease based on their results. Or, compare the learner's performance to a competitor. Based on the learner's ability to answer questions, they win the business or their competitor's do. This provides the student with real-world consequences and helps make the connection for why this material matters.

Ask the Character. Inserting a clickable character in the course to give students the ability to ask for help is another way to provide interaction for the learner. Script out characters who represent different viewpoints that the student might go to for help. This could be a co-worker, a manager, etc. When the learner is considering an option, they could click on the character and hear a 30 second sound bite that provides a different perspective on the issue. Some of the advice would be good, others less valuable. Use this type of interaction to encourage the mindset of asking other people for advice or consulting a resource to gain information.

Compelling Visuals. People like to explore an environment. Provide a compelling visual that allows the user to click on the image to learn more. We have used visuals to show cutaways of an interior wall for a motor home. The learner clicks on an icon to learn more.

The visual could be a map or picture of the facility, a poster or infographic. Using a compelling graphic allows the learner to explore the content in the order that makes sense to them.

My BIGGEST piece of advice moving forward...

There are so many ways to include interactions in your courses. The key to providing interactions is to know your audience and think about their needs as you develop the course. Before you ask the course designer to include an interaction, think about whether it adds value to the learning experience. A good rule of thumb is to include an interaction about every 3 screens.

Keep in mind that overly complicated interactions such as branching scenarios that go beyond 2 levels add to the cost of producing a course and may be unnecessary.

Summary:

- Use interactions to add value to your learners.
- Mix up the interactions within your courses; don't use the same clicks for everything.
- Include a knowledge check to reinforce important or complicated material.
- Give learners the opportunity to reflect upon or use the information to make decisions and receive feedback.

Mistake #7: He Knows Best

What is the mistake?

The mistake is trying to include all of the information you receive from a Subject Matter Expert or a previously developed course in your eLearning modules. SMEs play a key role in the developing your training program. They help you craft the learning objectives, create the content and review it for accuracy, and they provide you with valuable insights and feedback. Subject Matter Experts know a lot about their subject matter.

Why it's a mistake

Subject Matter Experts don't always know the best ways to teach what they know, especially when it comes to eLearning. And working with a SME can be a challenge as they can interfere and cause delays in getting a project completed on time.

Very often, the SME has moved on and is working at a higher level within the organization. They no longer work with new or inexperienced staff and have lost the perspective of what it's like to learn a new skill. They want to include far more information in the course than what is really needed to meet the course objectives and what the student needs to know to do their job.

The SMEs often consider all of the information they provide to be critical for the learner. They forget that it has taken them years to learn what they know. Their experience is shaped by their education and mistakes they have made along the way. They forget what it's like to be new to the subject area.

What are the consequences of making this mistake and how critical are they?

This can be a critical mistake. The learner can become frustrated and confused by the sheer volume of material that they are expected to learn. They can't distinguish between what they "need to know" and what is background or "nice to know" information.

If the student can't connect what they are learning to what they need to do on the job, they may fail. Or even worse, leave the organization.

For a membership organization, your students are paying for knowledge they can apply to their current position or to help them move up in the organization. If the material you are providing is confusing and too complicated, they will leave and look elsewhere. The benefit of an association is the applicability of the course content in the real world. It's important to get the level of content and quantity of information right.

Why and when do people tend to make this mistake?

One reason associations make this mistake is that they rely upon volunteer SMEs. A member comes to you with a course they believe would be great for your audience. You know they are the expert. Maybe you have even attended a live event where they were the presenter. But translating what they know to an eLearning course can be difficult.

Another reason why associations make this mistake is because they choose the wrong SME for the course. The first instinct is to choose someone with a lot of experience to be the Subject Matter Expert. An experienced SME comes with a lot of baggage. They may not be close enough to the learner to understand what they really need. They also carry with them years of bad practices, workarounds and war stories. They know too much for the beginner.

And still another reason is that the context is important to an expert, but it's not always relevant to the new learner. There is a balance between providing only the information the learner needs and the appropriate level of context the learner might not understand.

Associations also rely upon the SME to develop the course material in a timely manner. They don't establish clear expectations when working with the SME. There are no boundaries or limits placed on the course before it is developed.

Let me tell you a quick story to illustrate this point...

I was working with a top credit card company to develop a series of courses for their MBA students who were starting work with the company. As I interviewed each Subject Matter Expert, it was obvious that each one was sure the content they had to share was the most important. They felt strongly that everything in their PowerPoint presentation needed to be included. The time constraints for the course were considered unreasonable. For example, we had allotted 30 minutes to each SME to present the most critical information that the students needed to know. Getting the SMEs to agree to the limits was difficult, but ultimately the correct decision.

What should you do instead?

People don't necessarily care about what the SME knows. They only care about learning what they need to know to meet their own goals. Make sure you identify a SME that has worked day-to-day with the target audience. Organizations will recommend the person who has been doing the job the longest. The best choice isn't always the most experienced worker, but the most recently competent one—the newer person who remembers what it was like not to know how to do a task, and who remembers what it's like having to learn and what that entailed.

Help the SME focus on how the learner will use the information so you can build a learner-centric course. Focus on a performance-based outcome for your course that includes only the critical content and addresses the "What's in it for me?" factor. This is important in gaining and keeping the learners' interest.

Sometimes it helps to distinguish between tactical vs. strategic outcomes. In thinking tactically, the SME is focused on the content because “it’s the rule” versus thinking strategically, “if they don’t do it correctly, they won’t achieve their goals.”

Focus the modules on the actions the learner will take when performing their job. Create scenarios or case studies that are relevant and meaningful. Create a real world situation where the learner can apply the information. Walk the learner through a scenario where they get to make decisions and get feedback on how they apply the information. This strategy relies on the SME for guidance and information.

What should you do if you've already made this mistake? How do you fix it?

If you've already made this mistake, really look at the focus of your modules. Are you providing the right level of content for the learner? Go back to the SMEs and ask them to help you think strategically about each course. Make the changes quickly and re-launch the course if you must.

How do we prevent making this mistake moving forward?

It’s important to set the stage correctly when working with the Subject Matter Experts. Set expectations from the very beginning to ensure that anyone you are interviewing or obtaining information from understands the process and why you want to speak with them. Plan your interviews carefully taking into account:

- The purpose of the interview.
- How the information will fit in the final modules.
- The types of questions to ask.
- How long the interview will take.
- What kind of review or editing options the SME will be allowed on the final module?
- Who will conduct the interview?

Failure to set expectations can result in pushback from the SME and a lot of wasted time and effort on your part. Take time upfront to prepare for the interview. Understand why you are speaking with this particular SME. Think about:

- Why this person was recommended or chosen?
- What is this SME's specific area of expertise?
- How can you frame the conversation to ensure you keep your questions relevant and your interviewee engaged?

Conduct some research on the person and the topic in order to ask intelligent questions. Do not try to dazzle anyone with how much you know. The expert knows more than you.

Next **conduct the interview**. The interview is primarily a conversation. The more comfortable both of you are, the better the information you will receive.

Be respectful! But be ready to interrupt if the SME gets off-topic. It's your job to make sure you stay on topic and use the time you have together to your best advantage.

Record the interview if possible. And always take notes in case the recording fails. If conducting the interview in person, take notes in longhand. Opening a laptop or focusing on a screen can put a physical or psychological barrier between you and the SME and threaten the success of the interview.

Follow the conversation. Be ready to follow an interesting or relevant line of thought, even if it's not on your list of questions. However, be sure to address all of the critical questions on your list before ending the conversation.

Prepare an open-ended wrap-up question. This gives the SME a chance to add some final thoughts. This is often where you get the best information, the best quotes, or the best background material.

Here are some methods you can use to obtain great information from the Subject Matter Expert.

- Establish clear objectives and expectations when working with the SME.
- Bring them in on the project early.
- Stay on top of milestones and proactively communicate with the SME.
- Be sensitive to their workloads.

- Be clear on what you need and when you need it.
- Don't abuse the time you have with the SME.

The Subject Matter Expert can make or break your course content. Their real-world experience and expertise are necessary to great course design. Be respectful to be successful.

Any tools or insight to help people get results faster, easier, more efficiently?

An easy way to record your interviews is to use an iPad with a recording app. If you simply put the device on the table and forget it, your SME will forget it as well. Always ask permission before you record the conversation.

I have used Rev.com to transcribe the interviews. Currently they charge $1 per minute and their turnaround time has been exceptional.

If you don't have a Subject Matter Expert for a topic, use a service like ProNet or Reporter Connection to find an expert. You may need to pay a bit for their time. Always be sure the expert is providing their expertise in a way that the information can be used without paying royalties.

Prepare a simple template to help the SME provide you with the information you need. Use a basic training outline that covers the core objectives and asks questions that helps the SME share their expertise. Also ask how a new learner can practice using the information in the course and in the real work environment. This helps you to develop examples and scenarios later.

Here are some additional tips to use anytime you need to interview a SME.

Ask the right questions. Instead of asking "Does the learner need to know this information?" ask:

- Can you give me an example of when the learner would use this information?
- How often does that happen?
- What is the consequence if the learner doesn't know this / perform this?

Don't ask "What do you know?" Instead ask: "What decisions do you have to make?"

Also ask: "What are three common mistakes people make?"

Do your homework. Spend time researching and reading up on the topic before meeting with the SME. This gains you respect, increases your credibility and saves the SME time in walking you through the basic information.

If possible, be prepared with examples of your own. You can check your understanding of the material as you discuss your examples with the SME.

When walking through a procedure, try to avoid a screen-by-screen narrated reading. Instead, suggest or demonstrate other ways of presenting the information.

Remember, the SME already has a job. Don't expect endless, frequent meetings. Plan every conversation so you are getting all of the information in one setting. Don't call back endlessly because you forgot to ask something. Don't waste their time.

Build the relationship. The SME has information you need, so work to cultivate a good relationship. This will help you get the information you need. Be respectful. Appeal to their sense of expertise and mastery. Say Thank you.

My BIGGEST piece of advice moving forward...

The relationship and rapport you build with the Subject Matter Expert can make the difference between an easy working relationship and one that is always confrontational. If you are perceived as the expert in developing eLearning and they are the expert in their field, mutual respect builds. That means you are on an even footing and it makes the conversations mutually advantageous.

Summary:

- Pick the right Subject Matter Expert for the course you are developing.
- Do your homework and plan the module before you speak with the SME.
- Plan your questions and the interview to get the most out of the SME.
- Build rapport and establish a relationship with the SME.
- Always say thank you.

Mistake #8: Let's Build Them All At Once

What is the mistake?

This mistake is deciding to develop an entire series of courses all at one time. The idea is that if we are building one, why not just go ahead and develop all of them at the same time. We have everyone on board and we are ready to go!

Why it's a mistake

I am amazed at how often I get this request to develop many courses at one time. I have never had a project go well if I agree. The first problem is the time requirement to develop and deliver a course. It takes a considerable amount of time on the part of Subject Matter Experts, the Instructional Designer, Graphic Artist and Programmer to put together a great course.

Second, you won't have time to pilot a course to determine if you have met the needs of the organization and the learner. Does the look and feel work with your audience? Is the content appropriate? Are the interactions compelling? Have you picked the right media? Do you need to include video? Have you chosen the right narrator? All of these decisions can mean the difference between a module that is just good and one that your members will love.

Third, you won't be able to use a single Instructional Designer or Writer for all of the courses. This can be a problem when you are trying to build a brand and have the courses use the same tone and writing style. Writers, just like graphic designers, have a style. Mixing styles can be good but not when you are trying to produce a coherent, branded learning program.

What are the consequences of making this mistake and how critical are they?

The consequences of making this mistake depend upon the organization. For example, if you are a small association and the promise you make to your members is that you will hear from a variety of "experts" then it's not as critical. The audience is expecting variety and differences in the course style and design. They will still demand similarity in delivery and access, but the style can be different.

However, if you are a larger organization looking to brand your offerings and to provide certification, then it can be more important. Your learners will come to expect a certain look and feel as well as functionality. Standardizing how the user clicks through a course or accesses the video replays will be important.

Why and when do people tend to make this mistake?

Associations make this mistake because they don't really understand the commitment that needs to be made by the Subject Matter Experts and the Association Staff in meeting deadlines. Many times the deadline that the Instructional Designer sets is based on all of the elements being created on time. For associations and other organizations, deadlines can be seen as mere suggestions. If they meet them, great. If not, the Instructional Designer will just have to get it done any way they can.

Associations make this mistake because they have made a commitment to a higher authority, the Board of Directors, the Executive Director, etc. They think that by doing it all at once, they can actually save time and get the courses done more quickly. More often, doing it all at once can mean delays and missed deadlines or worse.

Let me tell you a quick story to illustrate this point...

One client wanted to develop multiple modules around a single topic. Multiple Subject Matter Experts were involved. The plan was that all interviews were to be done in February, the outlines completed by March, and the Storyboards completed by April. That would mean that all of the courses could be programmed by the end of August. As you can imagine, this project was never close to meeting its deadlines.

The Subject Matter Experts were not available in February and appointments had to be rescheduled frequently due to poor weather conditions and conflicting meeting schedules. The source material promised to the Instructional Designer was late, if they even received it.

The outline approvals were not completed in a timely manner. By June, only half of the module outlines were approved. The material in 2 of the modules was considered to overlap and 2 additional modules were requested. Not only that, but the approver obviously did not read the outlines or answer any of the questions posed by the writer about the content. By mid-June, only 3 modules were in storyboard format and had not been approved.

What should you do instead?

Before you create your first timeline, create a pilot program. Do one course or module from beginning to end. This allows the association staff to understand the process and their requirements in order to get the modules completed.

This allows you to educate the Subject Matter Experts, Association staff, and others about the process. It will help them understand what they need to do and how much time will really be required to fulfill their role.

This also allows you to spend the time to get the graphics created and to develop the branding or look and feel for your courses. When you send the course out for review, you can get feedback on everything from the overall look and feel, to the level of content, to the method of delivery.

Once you have the pilot program complete, make the changes based on the feedback you received. Incorporate all of your ideas into the Style Sheet. From this point, developing the remaining courses should be easier.

While you are piloting the course, you could be working with the Subject Matter Experts to gather all of the course materials and supporting documentation needed as you go forward.

Once the pilot program is ready, plan the remaining course development. You have the information you need to determine timeframes for writing, review and development. Not only will you be more accurate in developing the timelines, but the Association staff will be able to determine if they can realistically meet the proposed deadlines. A win for everyone.

What should you do if you've already made this mistake? How do you fix it?

Fixing this mistake is tough because you have already set the expectations and deadlines for course completion. Stop. Take a breath and figure out which course is most ready to be completed. Work on that one course to get it completely done so you can show a completed course to the Association Manager.

Hold a review session where you bring together learners, Subject Matter Experts, Course Developers, etc. and brainstorm any changes to the design. This is a good time to review the timeline commitments and plan the remaining courses. The key here is to do it all together. That ensures that everyone understands what their role is and the time requirements going forward. You may find that a few Subject Matter Experts will decline to be involved at this point. It's better to know that now rather than wait until it's critical to the project.

How do we prevent making this mistake moving forward?

It's simple. Never agree to take on multiple courses at once without first piloting one program. Follow your normal development process but complete only one course. Keep track of the time it takes from initiation through delivery and signoff so you can create a realistic timeline.

Share the results with the Association Manager or course owner so they understand what is truly involved. Then prioritize the courses for development and delivery. As you work on modules, batch similar content together and assign the content to one writer and developer.

Any tools or insight to help people get results faster, easier, more efficiently?

I often use a Google shared spreadsheet to track the progress of the modules. Use Google's Drive to share documents, images, spreadsheets and more. Here is a sample spreadsheet I use to keep track of each individual module.

Item	Responsible	Start Date	End Date	Actual Date	Status
Kickoff Meeting					
SME Interviews, Gather Materials (including video content)					
Determine Graphic Template					
Draft Outlines					
Internal Outline Review					
Draft Outlines to Outside Reviewer					
Receive Outline Feedback from Reviewer					
Draft Storyboards					
Receive Storyboard Feedback from Reviewer					
Edit Storyboards					
Prep for Video					
Video Acquisition					
Media Development					
Draft Programmed Course					
Receive Programmed Course Feedback from Reviewer					
Edit Programmed Course					
Finalize & Deliver Programmed Course					

Use a fill color in the status column to indicate progress: Red = Past Due, Green = Complete, Yellow = In Process. This makes it easy to identify what items are still open or past-due.

My BIGGEST piece of advice moving forward...

When asked to create multiple courses at one time, always do one as a pilot program so everyone understands the time commitment and resource requirements to complete the program. You may think you understand what's involved, but from my experience, the project never goes the way you think it will and delays are inevitable. It may seem like doing a pilot program will slow down the process, but it will actually speed it up.

Summary:

- Develop a pilot program for your courses to test out the method of delivery and course design.
- Make adjustments based on the feedback you receive.
- Manage your resources (time, money and people) wisely.

Mistake #9: If 20 Minutes Is Good, 60 Minutes Is Better

What is the mistake?

The mistake here is building your course using a single module that is 45-90 minutes in length. This happens frequently when you are taking a one-hour standup training course and turning it into an eLearning module.

Why it's a mistake

Today's working professionals have a lot on their plate and don't have much time to devote to training in their busy schedule. There are many distractions and shrinking attention spans that compete for the Association Member's attention. Not only that, your students may be forced to take your course as part of their job requirements.

Because of the distractions, waning attention spans and less than enthusiastic attendance requirements, you should seriously consider how long each eLearning module should be.

The research about attention spans sheds some light on how long our eLearning modules should be. First of all, let's define a learning module as an individual, focused lesson that represents a smaller portion of a longer course. The course then, would consist of many modules.

We are used to sitting in a classroom or lecture for 50-60 minutes at a time. In a study by Arizona State University professors, the adult attention span was reported to be 8 minutes. So if you are creating a module that is 50-60 minutes in length you are likely to be losing the audience attention.

Ralph A. Burns conducted a study on adult learners, finding that the bulk of information students were later able to recall was received during the first 5 minutes of instruction. (In Communication Studies we call that the "Primacy" effect.) Burns reported that the lowest level of attention occurred between the 15 and 20 minute mark.

Many eLearning professionals agree that the sweet spot for learning chunks is around the 10-15 minute range. Most people are satisfied with just the most basic information and the ability to get more as needed.

The recommendation is to keep your eLearning modules somewhere between 10 and 20 minutes long; with 30 minutes as the absolute maximum. It's better to have a number of modules within a course so learners can drop in and get the information as it's needed.

What are the consequences of making this mistake and how critical are they?

The consequences of making this mistake are, in fact, high. We risk losing our member's attention when we provide too much information or take too long to deliver the content. Learners want the information delivered in smaller chunks that they can use immediately.

Why and when do people tend to make this mistake?

When we try to use content that was created for another use, we often simply put the entire chunk of material into one course and call it quits. That 1 hour or 90 minute session may have multiple objectives that you are covering. The content rambles. The flow may not be solid. But we use it anyway because it's done.

The Subject Matter Expert may be insisting that everything must be in the course. They may not want to divide the content into smaller segments because they think that if someone doesn't take the entire course, they will be missing some key information.

And if you are required to take a course for Continuing Education Credits (CEUs), the requirement may be for a 60 minute course. Keeping track of the modules within the course and who has completed them before awarding the CEUs can be difficult.

Let me tell you a quick story to illustrate this point...

A government grant was issued to produce 30 minute modules for a training program. The grant specified both the time and the content to be included in each module. Unfortunately, when the Instructional Designer developed the modules, the material only took 15 minutes to cover. In the classroom, each module was between 30 and 60 minutes long. There were questions in the classroom and the instructor wandered off on tangents during delivery. Because of the time requirements, the Instructional Designer had to add additional information to pad the course. The Instructional Designer added Knowledge Checks and unnecessary examples and content just to meet the time requirements. The evaluations following the eLearning course were not very favorable. Learners felt that they were wasting a lot of time on redundant information.

What should you do instead?

Designing an eLearning course should be based upon sound Instructional Design principles and each course broken down in to smaller chunks of information or modules. How long the course should be depends upon these 3 key factors.

The Interest and Relevance of the Topic. How interested the learner is in the topic will determine how long their attention span will be. For example, if this is a topic of high interest, the learner may stay around for hours. If it's something they are required to participate in, their attention span will be much less. It will be important to tailor the lesson to the background and needs of your audience. Again, the needs assessment is critical to deciding how long to make your modules.

The types of interactions you use can also help lengthen the attention span of learners. If you provide interesting scenarios that reflect what the learner actually does on the job, you are more likely to keep their attention.

The Degree of Interaction. Putting your learners in control of the experience will engage them as active participants and holds their attention longer. This could be as simple as "click to choose your path" or as complex as engaging in a role playing exercise. Think about it. "Is it more fun to play a game or to watch someone else play?" Get your learners involved to keep their attention.

Course Quality. People judge a book by its cover and a course by its production values. Your learner's will notice if the interactions and production quality of the course are not professional. You should pay attention to the quality of the interactions and how the module appears on the screen, especially if you are addressing a professional audience. Ask yourself these questions:

- Is the material organized and does it flow smoothly?

- Are there visuals (pictures, graphs, icons) with each topic? Are they professionally created? Are they consistent throughout the module?
- Are the colors and the interface pleasing to the eye? Do they use the same color pallet? Are they consistent throughout the module?
- Is the narration clear? Did you use a professional or did a SME provide the voiceover?
- Is the module easy to navigate? Is the navigation intuitive? Is it obvious where to click?

Each of these production factors can play a part in whether your audience will be engaged in the course material.

What should you do if you've already made this mistake? How do you fix it?

If you've already developed a number of courses that are 30 minutes or longer, it would be a good idea to take a look at each one to determine if you can break the course into modules. For example, a 60 minute course could be broken down into four 15 minutes modules or six 10 minute modules.

Take a look at the production values. Have they met the criteria for a professional course? If not, redo them.

And finally, are there interactions built into the course that will keep your learner's interest. Sometimes just adding an interaction or two to a course can save it without doing much else.

How do we prevent making this mistake moving forward?

Anytime you are provided with a course that was originally delivered in another format, evaluate the material before you begin to develop the modules. For example, go through the content and identify:

- The course objectives.
- Topics within the course.
- Examples provided.
- Graphical elements (charts, pictures, icons).
- Handouts provided.
- Additional resources.
- Quiz or exam questions.

Use your results to develop an outline or mind map of the information. Look for logical breaks in the content or flow. Identify where you could insert an interaction. Identify sections or topics that seem to fit together well. Verify that the graphical elements are safe to include in your course. Are they "royalty free" or do you own the rights to them? Identify material in the course that seems to be redundant or unnecessary. Consider eliminating that information from the new modules.

Any tools or insight to help people get results faster, easier, more efficiently?

I'm a very visual person and like to see things in a way that I can move the content around. That's why I love mind mapping. I learned about mind mapping back in 1995 with *The Mind Map Book* written by Tony Buzan. Since then, I have used a variation of this method for almost every project I have undertaken. The process has evolved over time and now I use sticky notes and a white board or mind mapping software.

For each course objective, I create a sticky note and place it on the white board. Then as I review the course material, I write information about each topic on its own sticky note. As I post the notes on the whiteboard, I am free to look for associations and to move the content around until it makes sense. Since I have captured the content, I can even move it into a holding space or parking lot to be included in a different module.

You can be as creative as you like. Sometimes I use different colors to represent a topic or an activity. For example, yellow are the topics, green are the examples, and pink are questions I might have about missing content. I even have large size sticky notes to use as categories. I can organize the smaller sticky note topics under each larger category.

I use Mind Jet software to create mind maps if I need to share them with others. You can also use an "app" on your smartphone or iPad called CamScanner to take a picture and email the image to others. There are free options for mind mapping software as well.

My BIGGEST piece of advice moving forward...

Whenever possible, keep your eLearning modules somewhere between 10 and 20 minutes max. It's better to have a number of modules within a course so learners can drop in and get the information as it's needed. It also allows the learner to start and stop the course without having to start from the beginning. It also permits the learner to come back to a course and quickly review a selected piece of information when needed.

Summary:

- Keep the content of each module between 10 and 20 minutes.
- Limit the information in your eLearning courses to "need to know."
- Use interactions to keep your learner's interest.
- Make sure your production quality matches the audience's expectations.

Mistake #10: That Won't Cost Much

What is the mistake?

A mistake that many Association Managers make is underestimating the cost of developing eLearning programs for their organization. This includes developing content and assessment elements, visual and graphic elements, level of pre-course design preparation and mode of delivery for your content.

Keeping the costs down are important but you still need to develop courses that your Members will love.

Why it's a mistake

All eLearning is not created equal. There are many levels of online learning that you can use in your organization. The budget you create can vary widely depending upon the method of delivery, development tools, graphics, audio/video, and instructional design.

The level of preparation can also have an effect on the budget and resulting course design. Subject Matter Experts who present their courses in person are accustomed to filling in the blanks during the presentation. If you don't have detailed and complete notes for a presentation, it will take longer and cost more to develop the design and script.

The organization can also make a mistake if they use the wrong mode of delivery for their eLearning courses. Selecting the most expensive method is not always the most appropriate. If you only rely upon one method of delivery, you could be spending a lot more than you need to.

What are the consequences of making this mistake and how critical are they?

The consequences of making this mistake are critical. Underestimating a budget for your course design can mean the difference between offering several courses or only one. If you use your entire year's budget on one course, you are shortchanging your members. Being a good steward of the Association means using your funds wisely. Budgeting correctly is important.

Why and when do people tend to make this mistake?

Association Managers can make this mistake if eLearning is new to the organization because they are unfamiliar with what it really takes to develop eLearning courses. You may underestimate the upfront costs. The benefits to the organization come when you consider the time and travel savings for your members. It takes about ½ the time to present the same material online as it does to deliver it in person.

Budgeting can also be difficult if you are removed from your members. For example, if you have to rely upon an outside expert to provide the training materials it will be more costly than if you have staff or internal resources who can provide the expertise.

Budgets are usually developed based upon an "average person." There is no such thing as average. Your situation and staff are unique so using an average is going to be an estimate at best. Your budget estimates can be way off in either direction.

If you don't keep good records as you develop your courses, you won't know what your exact costs are. Especially if the training is complicated or new to the organization, the costs will generally not be correct in your initial budget. Keeping track of expenditures as related to the eLearning budget will be important going forward as you develop additional courses.

Let me tell you a quick story to illustrate this point...

I recently met with an organization to provide eLearning course development services for a series of modules on a single topic. The Manager assured me that they had all of their course materials from in-person training they present regularly. They had handouts and PowerPoint slides that would guide us in the module development.

Unfortunately, when we reviewed the information, the content on the PowerPoint slides were brief phrases and bullet points. There were no accompanying notes from the instructor and the handouts were incomplete and missing. The result was that the development took much longer than expected and resulted in additional charges to the organization. The writer had to do the research to complete the training materials as the SME was no longer available. Had we known upfront that the materials were in such poor condition, our estimates for the work would have been more accurate. Instead, we had to add a change request to the project in order to meet the needs of the project.

What should you do instead?

The following training cost guidelines can be useful when developing your budgets. These are only guidelines and will vary based on the type of training you are doing, the skill level of the design team, and your experience with eLearning.

Using video in your training programs is a great way to increase interaction and interest. If you use professional video production services, plan to spend $1,000 to $3,000 per finished minute of video. The cost varies depending upon the concept, the location, the talent used and any special effects. If professional video is not required, using today's digital cameras or an iPad can allow you to add video elements in your training programs for much less. The quality will not be quite the same, but you can do a good job at about $500 per minute.

Obtain professional graphic design services for your PowerPoint slides. Have a template made for your PowerPoint presentations. The money you spend getting a graphic designer to create a look and feel will go a long way in creating a professional image. Plan to spend $15 to $50 per slide.

Use photographs from a stock photo service or royalty-free images. Be sure to verify that you have the proper permissions to use a photo in your presentations. Photos can cost $1 to $100 each depending upon the size and the permitted use. If you have a location where using your own photos would make sense, hire a professional photographer to take images at your location. You will spend between $500 and $1500 for a day's photo shoot but the images will be yours to use whenever you want. This means you can use the photos again and again in any type of media because you own them.

Professional audio will cost between $25 and $150 per minute to produce. A lot depends upon the requirement you have for audio files. If the voice over artist provides one long audio session, it will take your programmer a long time to cut it up for use in your eLearning courses. Asking the professional to break the files into small chunks may cost a little more, but it will be easier for your developer. A good professional will ask your preference. Using a professional means your audio will be crisp and enunciated correctly. If however, you want a homier feel, you can produce the audio voiceover yourself. Be sure to use a professional microphone and software such as Audacity or Sound Forge.

If you will be providing a student guide or handouts of any kind, plan to spend four to eight hours for each ½ to 2 pages, depending upon the technical specifications.

For in-house Instructional Designers, eLearning Designers or Project Managers, plan to spend between \$28/hour (\$60,000/year) and \$38.46/hour (\$80,000/year). If you bring in an outside consultant, plan on spending between \$90 and \$125 per hour. You may be able to negotiate a flat project rate with a writer or instructional designer. Plan to spend between \$900 and \$2000 per 30 minute module for outline and storyboard development, depending upon the complexity of the material.

To estimate the development hours for your project, take these guidelines into consideration. These recommendations are found in several sources including Brandon-Hall and Chapman Alliance. For each hour of training, plan on the following development ratios:

Instructor Led Training (ILT)–Simple projects 22:1; Typical projects 43:1 and Advanced projects 82:1.

Basic eLearning Projects (Level 1)–Linear projects converted from PowerPoint – Simple projects 49:1, Typical projects 79:1 and Advanced projects 125:1.

Interactive eLearning Projects (Level 2)–interactive exercises, videos, audio, test questions – Simple projects 127:1, Typical projects 184:1, and Advanced projects 267:1.

Advanced eLearning Projects (Level 3)–simulations, games, award-winning interactions – Simple 217:1, Average 490:1, and Advanced 716:1.

As you can see, the experience you have and your own audit of time and materials will help you develop a budget that is more accurate. There are ways to reduce your costs, such as using Rapid Prototyping and reusable objects. Your first course is likely to be expensive, but the cost will decrease as you learn how to develop the courses more efficiently.

What should you do if you've already made this mistake? How do you fix it?

If you've already fallen into this trap, here's how you get out. If you decide that eLearning is the best mode to use for your modules, proceed with speed. Focus on straightforward, clearly communicated content. Spend your instructional development time creating a clear presentation of what you are trying to communicate. Focus your technical time on those few pieces that need to be refined. Employ standard tools for the mundane tasks like navigation, searching, and glossaries. Use a development checklist with smaller milestones that you can check off as they are completed.

Use rapid prototyping early in the project to keep budgets in check. Prototyping allows buy-in from the user experience group, content sponsor, and even the end users. If the prototype also incorporates all of the technical aspects of the final deliverable (coding, runtime versioning like Flash, LMS reporting, video, audio, graphics) the amount of rework and testing at the end of the development process will be greatly minimized. This will also allow for better overall acceptance of the content from end users and IT.

Skip expensive, time-consuming video production and professional voice overs. Use an iPad to create quick videos with amazing quality. Coach your SMEs in the best ways to speak on-camera instead of using professional talent whenever possible. In place of videos you can also take photos and connect the photos together in a montage with special effects such as fading in and out. Add a voiceover and you have a simulated video.

Learn how to use PowerPoint to quickly illustrate and present branching scenarios. Use hyperlinks to hidden pages so the end user will see only the active, pertinent page.

How do we prevent making this mistake moving forward?

Match training needs and content with the most appropriate method. For material with a short shelf-life and high level of interest consider rapid eLearning or a page on your intranet. If the training consists of introducing a new product or process, spend more money on interactive training that accomplishes results.

Develop the courses that meet your greatest need first. For example, develop the courses that take the most trainer time, most total learner time, or are the most expensive to hold in the classroom. Don't start with the courses that are easiest to develop.

Develop good courses from the start. Don't develop courses using poor design and functionality. Ineffective courses will not be successful and will cost you more in the long run.

If using content from an instructor led course, have the instructor write or script the information in the PowerPoint notes before you convert it to an online course.

Align your budget to focus on what is most important to the business. "What does the learner need to be doing differently to change performance?" instead of "What do they need to know?"

Ask the right questions before you begin any course development.

1. Short-term and long-term, what is your goal or objective to go online?
2. Will your programs be fully online, hybrid, or blended?
3. Who will manage the Learning Management System, Web-Based Training, or Computer-Based training?
4. Will the administration of the hardware, software, content and course development be managed in-house or outsourced?

Understand the requirements of your LMS system before you actually develop the first module. Identify the technical requirements, template demands, SCORM requirements and provide that information to your Course Developers. The last thing you want is to receive files that are too large or don't fit your system's requirements.

When narrating a course, have the SME first do a recording in a very casual way. Have that recording transcribed and edited for brevity and conciseness. Then do a final recording with the edited script. The result is a narration that sounds natural, not stilted. It captures the personality and style of the presenter and the way real people talk in general. The beauty of this is that the SME is not nervous trying to be perfect the first time around, and is much more comfortable when doing the real thing working from a polished script.

Use standardized file structure and naming conventions. This make it easier to reuse content objects, images and videos. Store the information in a central location and allow everyone on the development team access. There are always images and material than can be repurposed and reused which saves you money in development.

Any tools or insight to help people get results faster, easier, more efficiently?

Look for free online courses instead of developing your own. If the content is generic you may be able to customize the content by incorporating your own images and examples. Here are some resources to check out for free online courses:

Open Courseware Consortium (http://www.ocwconsortium.org) offers free college-level programs from recognized universities.

MIT Open Courseware (http://ocw.mit.edu)

SlideShare (www.slideshare.org)

Instructables (http://www.instructables.com)

Wikiversity (http://en.wikiversity.org)

Use Skype (www.skype.com) to present your courses and record the information. Use the free Skype plugin, Yugma Team Collaboration software (https://extras.skpye.com/1003/view) to turn Skype into a virtual classroom complete with whiteboard, application sharing, and file sharing.

If you have a training need that is not specific to just your own organization, there may be a course already available and it may be free. For example, if you are looking to provide financial education, the FDIC offers a very thorough financial education course that is free and has open access. Instead of creating your own course, provide a link directly to the FDIC's course through your LMS. Users can login to your LMS system and take the course. You track their participation. Many U.S. government agencies offer copyright-free content, classroom training guides and online courses.

Use online free learning objects such as those from:
Merlot (http://www.merlot.org),
iTunesU (http://www.apple.com/education/mobile-learning/),
YouTube (http://youtube.com),
Teacher Tube (http://www.teachertube.com), and
Intellicom (http://intellicom.com).

My BIGGEST piece of advice moving forward...

Spend time estimating your needs and creating a budget that is realistic. Consider whether you need to use professional talent in your videos and voiceovers or if you can use a SME instead. The level of interaction should also be considered in your budget planning. For simple courses, you will be able to get by with less. However, don't skimp just because your budget is small. Use your money wisely to get the best quality you can for the money you have to spend.

Summary:

- Develop a realistic budget for your course development efforts.
- Use realistic guidelines to estimate time requirements.
- Understand what elements need to be included and what are nice to have and budget accordingly.
- Make sure the delivery method matches the content you are providing.

Mistake #11: Because I Said So

What is the mistake?

Another mistake that Association Managers make is requiring that all instructional materials be developed using a specific software package. The software may be something that you are familiar with or the Association owns. Perhaps you have heard it's the best software available and believe it will mean your courses will be more effective if you use it. Perhaps you read about the software online or in a magazine and thought it looked great and would be "the product" to use to develop your content.

Why it's a mistake

Requiring specific software makes sense if you already own the software and have people who are familiar with how to develop programs using it. The problem is that the software you selected may not be the most appropriate one to use for the result you are seeking. For example, using Articulate Storyline to create a tutorial for how to use a new software package is overkill. A screen capture program such as Camtasia Studio can do the job more quickly and for a lot less money.

Or maybe you have been sold on the idea that all of your training needs to be done using professional video. The production company then, becomes the only resource you can use because they have the video b-roll files, the raw files and the on-screen talent. Making small changes can be expensive.

What are the consequences of making this mistake and how critical are they?

The consequences of making this mistake are high. Not only are you limiting the Instructional Designer when it comes to creating modules that are appropriate to the content, but you could be wasting resources developing content in the wrong media.

Why and when do people tend to make this mistake?

This mistake is made when an organization has purchased an expensive development tool and wants to ensure they get their money's worth. So every course they develop must use the tool, even if it's not the most appropriate one.

It may be that the consulting firm you hired to create the courses only uses one program for all their course development. You are relying upon their expertise to determine the relevant media and course software for your needs. The consulting firm may not have your best interests in mind when they make their software recommendations.

In addition, your course designers may only be familiar with one software program and therefore recommend you use it for all of your course development. It's human nature to resist change and move outside of your comfort zone. Course developers who are comfortable with one method may not want to consider anything else.

Let me tell you a quick story to illustrate this point...

I often work with other production companies to develop online courses for their clients. Each one has a favorite software they promote. The decision is often based on the software package they own. For example, one only promotes courses using Articulate Storyline because their programmers are familiar with it and use it daily. Another client requests Lectora be used because they own that software and have experience using it. These software packages are expensive to own and require experienced programmers to create the courses. It's cost effective for the production companies to only use one software package.

In many cases, using these software packages to develop the courses costs the client more money than they needed to spend. Not every course needs to be developed in these expensive packages.

What should you do instead?

Technology changes frequently. It can be difficult to keep up with all of the changes but choosing the appropriate software for the content and user needs is really important. You will find that you will often require multiple tools, depending upon the task. For example, you could use an authoring tool like Articulate and also need Camtasia for screen capture videos. Or you could use web conferencing software, quiz software and PDF handouts.

There are many different options to consider. Here are some basic questions to get you started.

What type of modules will you be developing? Strictly from a PowerPoint presentation? A replay of a Webinar or Teleseminar? How to demonstrations? Procedures? Product offering? Soft skills training? Expert advice? Question and Answer? Understanding the types of modules you will be building will help you select the appropriate software.

What kind of interactions will you use? Do you need branching scenarios where the user can choose their path through the module? Will simple page-turning interactions be sufficient?

Will you include different types of media? For example, will you embed video or audio into your modules? Will you need to include graphic elements such as charts, graphs, or pyramids?

Do you have a budget for software? What is it? Using the software you currently have is one option. For example, PowerPoint can be imported into authoring software or made interactive using internal links. There are also free or low cost solutions with basic functionality that might be enough to get you started.

How will your courses be delivered? Do you have a Learning Management System (LMS)? If not, will the courses be delivered from your website? How will you keep track of participation? There are many paid and open-source LMS systems available. You will need to understand the capabilities and limitations of your LMS before you develop the courses.

Do you need to include a graded quiz? Some organizations require that learners pass an exam to receive credit for the course. How will you track quiz scores and provide certificates of completion?

Are you providing Continuing Education Units? How will you track participation and maintain records? CEUs are often based on a mandated time in the course/classroom. This may require that your courses be of a certain length. How will you ensure your participants complete the entire training and not just skip to the end?

Do your courses need to be ADA or SCORM compliant? Does your software provide compliant courses? Are all of the elements compliant?

Will your courses be accessed from a mobile device? Some software programs can be viewed on multiple platforms, other cannot. Are your courses "responsive" meaning that they can be resized automatically based on the device that is being used. More and more people are using their tablets and smartphones to access training modules. Can your software handle quizzes if needed?

What should you do if you've already made this mistake? How do you fix it?

If you've already purchased an authoring software, be sure you understand its capabilities and limitations. Most people only know a few of the features of any software they buy and don't make use of all of the features and functions.

Take a look at some additional options that can be incorporated into your learning programs. Many are low cost or no cost to get you started. There are also free trial periods for many which will allow you to try before you buy.

Be open to options and push your training vendors to justify their selections based on the needs of your audience and members. Don't rely upon one method for all of your course development efforts.

How do we prevent making this mistake moving forward?

Be sure to understand the capabilities of each of the software packages you are considering for purchase. The best software will be the one that works best for you. Here are some additional things to consider when looking for software. This is not an exhaustive list.

Price. How much do licenses cost? How many licenses will you need? For example, Captivate can be purchased for about $900/license. Studio and Storyline for $1400 and Lectora $1600. There are free versions of software that may meet your needs. How is the support? Is it live? Is support extra? Are there forums and chat rooms that support the software? This can really be important for new users.

Ease of Use. Is the software intuitive or will there be a long learning curve? Many times if you know how to create more than basic slides in PowerPoint, you will be able to learn to use the eLearning development software. Be sure the features you want to use are included in any software package you purchase. You might find that there are many features that you do not need that add to the learning curve and development costs.

Graphics and Animations. PowerPoint has many features included that users are unfamiliar with. Using the PowerPoint features may be enough in many cases. Look for programs that allow you to create animations and use imported graphics easily. You will want to be able to create gradients, crop and rotate images, and apply dropdown shadows at the very least.

Interactivity. What options for adding interactivity are included? Are there templates or do you have to develop the programming yourself? How many layers deep can you go when building a scenario?

Quizzes and Assessments. What types of quiz questions can you use? How are the answers displayed? Can you rotate the questions and responses? How are quiz results captured and displayed? Can you develop custom logic?

ADA/SCORM Compliance. This refers to the international and national standards for design and navigation. If this is important to your organization you will want to know what features are and are not 508-compliant.

Mobile. Is your software capable of playing on mobile devices? For example, if you are publishing on an iPad or iPhone, you will need a player specifically for these products or the ability to publish in HTML5.

Any tools or insight to help people get results faster, easier, more efficiently?

Here are some favorites and top-rated software that you should consider when developing your courses in your organization.

dominKnow Claro features SaaS, online/offline sync with their own tool and via a supported LMS, templates, multiple languages, objects, branching, collaboration, HTML5 output. No tech skills required so good for instructional designers and eLearning developers. http://www.dominknow.com/

Articulate Storyline is geared toward instructional designers and eLearning developers and will require some technical skill. A great tool that includes templates, branching, simulations and multiple outputs. Also includes assessments/quizzes and other graphical elements.
https://www.articulate.com/products/storyline-overview.php

ZebraZapps is geared toward instructional designers and eLearning developers. Uses a different layout structure than that found in other authoring tools. Its SaaS based, SCORM supported and more. Could be used by someone with limited tech skills. https://zebrazapps.com/

CourseLab is ideal for instructional designer and eLearning developers. The commercial version includes templates, VML/SVG vector objects, avatars, limited object library, limited screen capture and multiple languages. Supports many browsers including Chrome, Opera, Safari, IE and Firefox. http://www.courselab.com/

Epic GoMo Authoring tool is ideal for mobile. Features include the ability to view offline or via a native HTML web app, and preview feature for iPad. Android, iPad and Blackberry support, SCORM and assessment tools. http://epiclearninggroup.com/us/platforms/gomo-learning/

Brainshark showcases PowerPoint and has a strong enterprise version that includes features such as branching, assessment tool, text-to-speech converter, social media links, output to MP4, certificates and SCORM. http://www.brainshark.com/

Easygenerator features include adaptive learning, collaboration, scenario builder, SCORM, question pool/assessments and SaaS. If you use this program you may want the fee-based product. https://www.easygenerator.com/

iSpring Solutions. iSpring Suite provides an add on product to PowerPoint. It has many of the capabilities of Articulate Studio at a lower cost. New releases include a PowerPoint to HTML 5 output. http://www.ispringsolutions.com/

GoToWebinar. This screen capture video/audio conferencing tool is ideal for capturing content presented in a Webinar or Teleconference. The software can record the session which can then be edited in any editing software and uploaded to an intranet or internet site. http://www.gotomeeting.com/online/webinar

TechSmith Camtasia Studio. This is not always considered an authoring tool since it captures screens to produce videos. It has a mobile piece and allows the user to create professional videos that can be hosted on websites and embedded into other programs. http://www.techsmith.com/camtasia.html

Go! Animate is not an authoring tool but enables you to create scenarios with actors/avatars which can be lip synched with your voice. Each character can be fully customized right in the product.

Output is to MP4 which means you can use it in any authoring tool that support it. http://goanimate.com/

Udutu is a free online authoring tool with an option for an LMS. If you are just starting out and want to create your first training module, this might be the right choice for you. http://www.udutu.com/

My BIGGEST piece of advice moving forward...

Make sure the software you are using to develop your eLearning programs meets your needs and budget. Don't limit your development to one tool that a consultant recommends. Do your homework and be willing to expand how you think about development. PowerPoint might be the only tool you need when starting out. Adding additional features and software can be done when you are ready and have experience with the process. Technology is always changing and new products are offered and old programs are updated. What you are currently using may not be the best tool to meet your needs today.

Summary:

- Evaluate your needs and the types of courses you deliver to identify the best tools for your organization.
- Don't let a consulting firm dictate your options based on their needs.
- Try out different options before you spend money on an expensive tool.

Mistake #12: Show Me The Money

What is the mistake?

The mistake here is not using the courses you have created to generate non-dues revenue for your Association. You spent a lot of resources (both time and money) to put together a great learning package for your Association members and then don't fully utilize the courses to bring in non-dues revenue.

Why it's a mistake

Associations are always looking for ways to increase retention, attract new members and generate non-dues revenue. Having great courses for your members goes a long way to meet those goals. But offering your courses only to members can limit your revenue. Instead, think of ways that you can use your developed courses as a marketing lead generation tool and revenue source.

What are the consequences of making this mistake and how critical are they?

The consequences of making this mistake can be high. Many Association Managers are tasked by their Boards to generate income outside of dues in order to support the vision and mission of the organization. That means putting on events and fundraising efforts. Repurposing your training content can be a way to generate revenue that is less costly than planning and running other fundraising efforts.

Why and when do people tend to make this mistake?

This is a mistake that is made in a lot of organizations, not just an Association. It's difficult to see that what we create can be repurposed and reused in a variety of ways. If you don't have a lot of experience marketing your products it can be challenging to even consider doing so.

Small and medium-sized Associations don't have the staff that can focus on marketing the training programs to their members, much less offering their training to others. Developing an online learning program requires some planning and expertise to do it correctly. But once in place, can be easily offered to others creating additional programs and products you can sell.

Association Managers don't always understand how these training programs can generate additional revenue without a lot of IT support and expense. The internet is changing rapidly and it's easier than ever to promote your programs in a variety of ways that don't cost a lot or require a great deal of expertise. You just need to learn some basics and connect with knowledgeable people.

Let me tell you a quick story to illustrate this point...

I have a good friend who is a Pet Behavior expert. She often creates content for Associations and other pet related organizations. She is highly sought for her speaking and training services. She also markets her training programs online. One way that an Association can take advantage of the revenue-generating aspect of her classes is to offer them free to members as a member retention or acquisition tool. She also offers her courses to Association members as a paid training with revenue sharing for the Association. The Association gets a portion of the revenue for the training course and sometimes commissions for future product sales. The benefit to the expert is that they have access to your membership list to promote their courses. The benefit to the organization is they have access to the expert's contact list for potential new members. This typically is a win-win for both parties.

What should you do instead?

One of the easiest ways to promote your courses is to offer free webinars. This is by far the easiest way to build your prospect list, build relationships with your current members and sell your products and services. The webinar can simply answer the most frequently asked questions around a topic. At the end you promote your course as the "How To" solution. Advertise your webinar using Facebook and send emails to your current membership and prospect list. If you don't have a list, you can build one using this method.

Spend some time developing a marketing plan that takes into consideration your current expertise. This would be a good time to bring in a marketing consultant that is familiar with online marketing techniques. Once you have a system in place, it's easy to replicate the system for each course you develop.

What should you do if you've already made this mistake? How do you fix it?

If you've already created courses or modules, put together a marketing plan/system and execute it. There are many ways to market your courses so you need a plan. That way you can identify what works and what doesn't. Organizing a marketing system doesn't have to be complicated. Here's some ideas for an approach you can use.

The first thing is to **create the infrastructure**. This is the system you set up so you are ready to implement the marketing plan. It doesn't matter yet about advertising or social media. That comes later. This is the lead generation aspect of marketing.

Put together a "lead magnet." This is the item that you promote that motivates the prospective member to opt-in to your mailing list to receive it. This could be the free webinar, a white paper, free report or video. You must have a really cool, intriguing headline and title to attract attention.

The next item is a **one page website** that promotes the lead magnet OR a VERY big promotional section on your website landing page that draws attention to the free offer. I suggest the one page website because it's easier to promote later.

Next you need to develop a **series of messages** that are sent out to your current and prospective members that promote this lead magnet offer. The messages should give away some of your best tips, tactics or strategies. Don't worry about giving away the best stuff. There is a lot of competition for your audience so you need to be seen as a credible and trustworthy source of information. These messages may be shared later with a SME to share with their list.

This leads to the **irresistible offer**. This is a page that sells the prospective member on why they should purchase your course, membership or other service you are offering. There are a lot things that go into this page but this is the sales letter. It can be done using video, text or a combination thereof. Include testimonials, a guarantee and a way to purchase your course or products.

Now you are ready to **begin the promotion**. This is all of the activities you will use to promote the free offer and get people to opt-in and become a subscriber. Most of your new members will come from your group of subscribers, members and buyers so you want to be sure to capture their names and email addresses. This is where you would use an AutoResponder service such as aWeber, Constant Contact or MailChimp to automatically send out your emails.

The promotion includes such things as internet advertising, social media, blog posts, joint ventures with your SMEs, public relations and more. The important thing is to get your lead generation activities done before you begin the promotion.

How do we prevent making this mistake moving forward?

Get in the habit of developing a webinar around the topic of your courses. Answer the burning questions your audience has about the topic. Create a PowerPoint presentation and present the webinar using a web conferencing software such as GoToWebinar.com, FreeConferencing.com, or Skype.com. Be sure to promote your new course at the end. Record the session. Do some minor editing to the recording and save it as an MP4 video, MP3 audio or both. Now the fun begins!

Using your webinar, you can have the recording transcribed. You can strip out the audio to create an MP3 file with just the audio. You could create a checklist or handouts to share with the audience. You could turn the transcription into a Kindle book or white paper. You could use a portion of the webinar as your lead magnet. You could sell the replay. There are many ways to use the webinar content to provide value to your members and prospective members and generate income.

Any tools or insight to help people get results faster, easier, more efficiently?

Develop your webinar around a topic that is of high interest to your audience and that leads naturally to your course offering. Use this information to develop your web presence for the opt-in and sales pages. A great way to get professional website pages is to use Optimize Press. http://www.optimizepress.com/ Their templates and security features are great and the cost is a one-time fee as opposed to a monthly charge for similar services.

I use GoToWebinar to promote and host my webinars. Their recordings are good quality and can be easily edited using a variety of editing software. The advantage is that when people sign up for the webinar, they automatically get reminders. This helps to ensure attendance at your presentations. You can also export attendee information into your AutoResponder for follow up later.

To transcribe my webinars, I send the audio file to Rev.com. They do a great job and get the transcription done very quickly, usually the same day or within 24 hours. Their prices are very reasonable and they can transcribe multiple voices.

My BIGGEST piece of advice moving forward...

My biggest piece of advice is to promote your courses using a Webinar. This will allow you to build relationships with prospective members and to offer your courses and ancillary materials to increase your non-dues revenue.

Summary:

- Use a Webinar to promote your courses and build relationships with potential and current members.
- Set up a marketing system to ensure you are doing everything you can to promote your eLearning courses.
- Develop additional products to generate non-dues revenue and provide value to your members.

Conclusion

Now that you understand the 12 mistakes that sabotage your education programs and how to avoid them, let me share with you my checklist.

This checklist contains specific questions to help you avoid the eLearning mistakes discussed in this book. All you have to do is just ask these questions before you develop your next eLearning course. If you answer "Yes" to each question, except for #7 and #11, then you are good to go!

1. Do I have a strategy and plan for developing an eLearning program in my organization?
2. Does my training staff have the skills and experience to develop eLearning courses?
3. Do my course developers use sound instructional design or are they caught up in the "latest" methodology, even if it's not right for our members?
4. Do my course developers create course plans, outlines and storyboards before sending the material to the programmer?
5. Do we have a Style Sheet to guide all of the development of our eLearning courses and do we follow it?
6. Does the instructional designer plan the interactions in the courses to engage the learners?
7. Do the Subject Matter Experts dictate the course content?

8. Do we create a pilot of the first course in a series to ensure we have met the needs of our learners?
9. Are our courses divided into small chunks of information as opposed to delivering one long course?
10. Do we have a realistic budget that takes into consideration all of the recommended resource elements and requirements?
11. Do we require all courses be developed using a single software or delivery method?
12. Do we have a marketing plan to ensure our courses generate non-dues revenue?

Final Thoughts

Choose 3 of the mistakes that you need to correct and fix them first. In other words, you don't have to fix all of these at one time. Identify the ones that are the easiest for you to fix and concentrate on those first. Build some momentum for yourself.

Don't tackle the hardest ones until you have had some success fixing the easiest ones. Allow yourself and your staff to celebrate a success. It will make it easier to continue to build on that success and tackle those additional mistakes.

Then choose 3 more and fix those until you have finished fixing them all. Start small, but do something every single day.

I hope you enjoyed this book. I know that by paying attention to these 12 mistakes you'll be able to improve and get better results from every eLearning course you provide to your members.

Next Steps

Your next steps are pretty straightforward and simple. Do everything you can to avoid making these 12 mistakes!

Use the checklist to ensure you are doing the best you can for your members. Always strive to provide your members with the best quality, up-to-date, easy-to-access courses that you possibly can.

Don't Get Left Behind

A Personal Invitation from Deborah Miller

Because you bought my book I'd like to invite you to visit my blog and subscribe to receive updates so you can get the practical insights, tips and tools that I find valuable when providing eLearning services to my clients. I have also created a page on this website with all of the products and links I included in this book as an easy reference for you.

If you want to learn how to create eLearning courses that members love, explode your credibility with your members, and generate non-fee revenue, then here's what I'd like to invite you to do. Go ahead and log on to www.eLearningSecrets.com and sign up for a free account. It takes about 30 seconds and could very well revolutionize the results of your eLearning courses.

That means you'll be able to get all the latest developments in eLearning, as well as my latest tips, tricks and tools to leverage with your own eLearning courses (no matter what industry you are in).

Again, signing up is easy and FREE. Point your web browser to www.eLearningSecrets.com and sign up for a free account (we promise never to spam or share your name with anyone).

So if you enjoyed this book and want to take your eLearning courses to the next level, head on over to www.eLearningSecrets.com right now and get onboard for free.

Deborah C. Miller Bio

My name is Deborah C. Miller and I have been writing and developing training since 1992 for a wide variety of organizations. I started out developing and delivering stand up training and progressed through all of the different types of training: Experiential, Active, Accelerated, Ropes, CBT, WBT, Agile, Rapid, Webinar, and much more.

In 2000, I traveled the country teaching insurance agents how to use a new client management software program.

In 2005 I was introduced to eLearning and created my first CBT training program for a medical facility.

In 2007 I became the Director of Education for a small consulting firm and developed online learning courses for their clients.

Along the way I have written eLearning programs and created eLearning strategies for non-profits, manufacturing, financial services and health care organizations; small businesses and Fortune 200s.

My clients hire me because I am a practical, down-to-earth professional who works with their organization to solve problems and get results. I'm there to help them tell their story, not to sell them what they don't need. Because I am a small business, I can provide high value professional services at a reasonable cost.

I created many eLearning courses over the years which means I have real-world experience and can work with your staff to create great eLearning programs for your organization.

In my role as eLearning consultant, I always recommend starting with an analysis and assessment of past and current educational programs. We often spend time completing a Needs Analysis/Survey or Assessment to determine the best path to take to achieve your goals.

Bottom Line: I'm all about helping my clients to solve THEIR problems in a practical and common sense manner.

For speaking or consulting inquiries, or to get all the updates on eLearning, you can contact me through my website at http://www.eLearningSecrets.com.

Additional Publications by Deborah C. Miller

Available from Amazon.com